conversation
made easy

conversation
made easy

by
ELLIOT RUSSELL

Foreword by
Melvin Powers

Melvin Powers
Wilshire Book Company

12015 Sherman Road, No. Hollywood, CA 91605

Published by special arrangement
with Elliot Right Way Books—England

Printed in the United States of America
ISBN 0-87980-024-0

FOREWORD

There is growing concern today about the almost inhuman desire of many of our citizens not to let their lives become involved with the lives of others, but it would be incorrect to say this feeling is inherent. Most of us would like to be gregarious, but the world is approaching full circle, which is to say that uncounted numbers of the world's inhabitants have reverted to the ancient custom of seeking no man as a friend until he has proved he is not an enemy.

It is not surprising that this mass retreat into privacy is occurring because each day our mass mediums of communication afford fresh evidence of violence and guilt by association. We are all aware, whether nations or individuals are involved, that today's entente may be tomorrow's misalliance, and we do not wish to become a partner or witness to anything that may cause us inconvenience at the least or death at the most.

We had an example of both recently when a number of people stood by, offering no help, while a young neighbor girl was murdered, while a few miles away an onlooker went to the help of a complete stranger and was stabbed to death for his courage and unquenchable spirit of brotherhood. If you know you would fall into the former classification of individuals, you should feel a twinge of conscience even though, as the author of this book points out, you have been conditioned to your reaction by following precepts that have been drilled into you from the earliest time you could comprehend the meaning of two major warnings that are given to most American children.

How many of us can ever forget the oft repeated parental admonishment, "Don't speak to strangers," or its variation for persons of all ages, "Mind your own business." These twin pieces of advice are given so frequently that they are commonplace, but valuable as they may be in certain situations, they may also account for a seriously withdrawn personality.

Neither Freud nor Pavlov is mentioned by Elliott Russell in this excellent book, but he pays tribute to the accuracy of some of their theories and clinical observations. For example, the child who has been told, almost from birth, not to speak to strangers may have difficulty striking up a conversation with someone he does not know even though the early advice has been invalid for many years. In these cases shyness is equated with fear, a devastating emotion that can cripple the personality.

The early fear, if the child was given a rational explanation, stemmed from the fact that he might be kidnapped or done bodily harm, but his adult emotion is much more likely to be due to the fear of his friendly overtures being rejected. When one remembers that Pavlovian conditioning results when an action or philosophy is continually reinforced (Don't speak to strangers. Mind your own business.), it is not surprising that millions of people have difficulty in communicating with others and forming friendships.

The author of this book does not neglect to mention these conditioned barriers to conversation, but he lists a multitude of ways they can be surmounted. These specific ways, however, take second place to the injunction that each person must have "a clear mental picture of the kind of person he would like to be" before he can begin achieving his goal. This is, as we have discovered in several recent books, the concept of Self-Image psychology.

We are not born, Mr. Russell says, with the ability to be good conversationalists. It is an art that must be cultivated, and most people can use all the help they can get. It might be added that people must learn to walk before they can run, and the knack of making so-called "small talk" must be mastered before one can go on to more intimate, technical or intellectual conversations.

To be truthful, the much disparaged "small talk" has always produced more friendships than dialectical discussions which are apt, more often than not, to result in argument. This does not mean, as friendship progresses, that controversial subjects cannot be discussed without endangering the cordial relationship, but if the friendship is valued inflammatory subjects will be approached with caution.

Politics, for instance, and friendship make strange bedfellows, and if you persist in discussing the former you may lose the latter. Mr. Russell thinks some subjects should be avoided among friends, and he thinks there are many times when silence is a positive virtue. This contrasts decidedly with the many books which offer their readers just enough superficial knowledge so that they may converse glibly in areas about which they know practically nothing.

Such persons, far from attaining their objectives, sustain twin disasters. They lose the friendship of those who know nothing about the subject, but become angered if they think they are being patronized, and they lose the friendship of those who are really knowledgeable in the field, recognizing the paucity of the pretender's knowledge.

There is great value in knowing a little bit about as many things as possible, but only if that little knowledge is used to elicit further information from those who are more learned in the field. This is an easy way to learn and make friends at the same time because even the most intellectual individuals are human enough to want recognition.

Sometimes this recognition of another has strange results. Samuel Johnson (1709-1784), a British author and lexicographer, was famous in his day, but our present dictionaries give more space to his biographer, James Boswell (1740-1795), although it is admitted that Dr. Johnson would have to share billing with more people than Boswell. The point is, however, that Boswell's "portrait" of Johnson has stood the test of time as well as Johnson himself.

In mentioning Johnson and Boswell, the author of this book brings out a facet of Johnson's personality which should give hope to all those who feel speechless when confronted with someone famous or one they believe to be their superior. Despite his ability to speak brilliantly on a variety of subjects, Johnson encouraged others, especially young men, to speak and "paid due attention to what they said."

It is impossible now to know exactly why Johnson made this remark, but we know why it might be attributed to any famous scholar of today. Because of specialization, all scholarly pursuits tend to become closed systems which reject any new ideas that cannot be fitted into the conventional framework of what has already been built. But a truly great man is not afraid to tear down the whole edifice of his discipline if a new idea indicates his old structure is obsolescent.

Strangely enough, such revolutionary ideas are most likely to come from outside the system in much the same way as Einstein, a mathematician, elaborated a new theory of physics. He was not a specialist in physics, but this was helpful because he approached the subject with an open mind, unmindful and uncaring of what was "proper" thought.

It may seem a long way between your ideas and those of Einstein, yet large corporations pay tribute to the so-called average man's ideas by placing suggestion boxes throughout their facilities. Out of those boxes have come solutions that stumped the experts, and those solutions have come largely because the authors did not know that what they proposed was "impossible."

In this book, Mr. Russell goes far beyond that basic type of conversation which is limited to the weather and inquiry about the state of the other's health. Repartee, wit, humor, aphorisms and epigrams are discussed, all with the use of anecdotes which the author considers so important he devotes a chapter to the subject.

Unquestionably, the seeming ability of Abraham Lincoln to summon up an anecdote to illuminate every situation contributed greatly in enlarging his circle of friends, and ensure his place in history over others who do not stir one's imagination. Anecdotes did not sustain him while the Union was being torn asunder, but he used them to illustrate his meaning during the darkest days this nation has endured.

Everyone, of course, cannot coin aphorisms or epigrams (as Russell correctly notes, there is a difference between the two) with the ease of an Oscar Wilde, but every person can make it a point to learn something new each day, thus increasing his chances to maintain a mutually interesting conversation. Reading is an excellent way to do this, and it should not stop with the daily newspaper.

Above all, perhaps, a good conversationalist must be sincere. He must be as interested in what other people have to say as he is in putting forth his own ideas and opinions. Self-centered individuals make poor conversationalists and few friends because they seek to dominate every dialogue. The unchecked ego is quickly apparent to all.

Curiously, the good conversationalist does not have to speak with apparent ease or lack of effort. It is human nature to distrust the "born orator." He usually has too much conviction, and too little concern for others. A sincere belief, no matter how tortured the manner in which it is delivered, is apt to be accepted at face value. Here, again, is another count against glibness.

If you cannot attract listeners by being yourself, it is time to change your personality — not what you are trying to say. The person who is genuinely interested in others will find he says the right things automatically. This means that opinions less than expertly expressed by persons who are unselfish will be better received than the most brilliant remarks of those who continually seek to be the center of attraction.

In my final remarks about this valuable book, I would be remiss if I did not mention its delightful literary style which is in the best tradition of the many English writers quoted. One poet cited by Mr. Russell is William Cowper (1731-1800) whose fame remains undiminished, perhaps because he followed his own advice given in the lines following:

"A tale should be judicious, clear, succinct,
The language plain, the incidents well linked;
Tell not as new what everybody knows,
And, new or old, still hasten to a close."

Best wishes and good luck to you in your attempt to become a better conversationalist.

Melvin Powers

12015 Sherman Road
No. Hollywood, California 91605

INTRODUCTION

THERE are two main kinds of conversation, that interesting and often exciting talk of the experts, into one of whom it will be my aim to develop you—and what is called small-talk or introductory conversation which breaks the ice.

This latter is of importance, particularly to the shy, and I will try to show you how to accomplish it by giving hints and examples. Without it, the road to greater things is partially closed.

In an age of Television and Cinema we are in danger of losing the art of talk and with it much more. For, through conversation, we find friends and keep old friends and are not old friends often the best? In time all artificial entertainments bore and weary but true companions, to whom you can talk without second thought, are never dull.

Conversation is the human attribute—no animal can talk or laugh—and we do not even realise what we miss if we are unable to indulge freely in it. We miss more than half of the pleasure of life and nobody can afford that.

CONTENTS

CHAPTER I

BREAKING THE ICE

BEFORE a man can become a conversationalist in any company, obviously he must know enough tricks to break into that company, that is, unless he has been properly introduced.

To-day people often forget to introduce and introductions are less common, yet many people fail to find friends or conversation because their small-talk is defective. This book is not written for experts so I make no apology for being elementary in this chapter. Shy people should find knowledge here which is useful.

People are not born with an 'easy manner'. To break the ice in trains, clubs or when you like is not simple for some, because, like many important things in life, we are not taught how in school. Yet what is more delightful than to be able to talk and possibly become friends with those whom you like the look of. Let's be honest about it. Have we not all seen people at the race meeting or sat next to someone in the train with whom we would like to speak but felt we dare not? Convention, etiquette or what you will stood in the way. All right—even before Ovid told us how to start a conversation with the pretty lady in the arena, people have been successfully introducing themselves to strangers.

It's an art, make no mistake about that. It's an art in which the Americans are ahead of the British, from whom the latter can learn. But even in the States are shy people who miss golden opportunities.

The humbug of the whole thing began long ago when we were told "Don't speak to strangers". The girl who tries to "get off" at the seaside by dropping her handkerchief may be a fiction of the past and would today be very suspect, but wherever there are young men and girls some way will be found of meeting and don't forget many good friendships have been made unconventionally.

The classic (and true) example of the English nobleman who, seeing a pretty girl on the platform as the train passed, pulled the communication cord and eventually married her is only an exaggerated case of what happens daily in all classes of society.

Most of us judge people on sight, sometimes, but less often than you think, wrongly, and owing to the unwritten laws of good manners, theoretically we can do nothing about it when we see someone we like. Fortunately, in practice, there is a great deal you can do.

SMALL TALK

As a first necessity, whether one wishes to speak to the person waiting with you to be served in the shop or whether you want to introduce conversation to a bored and silent company in a railway carriage, small-talk is essential.

This requires study. Subjects such as the weather, apart from being trite, are apt to be suspect. A little harmless subtlety is excusable if the ends justify the means! The art of small talk or introductory conversation can be learned in theory by reading the "gossip columns" in the daily and weekly papers and magazines. Memorise a lot of interesting facts and information about people and things, so that you build up a store on which to draw.

In practice, opening a conversation requires experience, and at first you will probably fail miserably. You may even be snubbed, but don't worry over that because in time you will learn how to handle many differing occasions and types of people. It is not easy to formulate rules because few situations are similar.

This may be said, however. Always be polite, diplomatic and careful not to offend. Always be able to retreat if you get the wrong reaction. Always try to find some topical way of starting as this stands a better chance. Always be an opportunist.

To illustrate the last point first, in the case of the proverbial railway carriage conversation (or lack of it) something usually happens which provides an opening for the skilful negotiator. It's quite simple when the train stops between stations. You break silence with an "excuse me" as you move to look out of the window. The crack in the ice made by this remark makes it easier to break through entirely. When you tell the other passengers you "can't see a thing" or that "the 3.15 is just ahead" they will happily accept it. You could lead on by asking if anyone objects to the window being left open. From this point various openings can be made. Others are likely to talk back or at this stage, even the weather or sport will not seem out of place, if you can't think of anything more exciting.

I purposely gave a simple illustration. In many situations these very straightforward methods are by far the best. This applies especially between the same sex. A man can ask another man in the golf club for a game without a thought. At tennis clubs mixed players can politely invite each other for a game, when there are four players. Anglers by the riverside invariably chat about their sport or the lack of it.

To a great extent the problem of speaking to strangers of the same sex or to a number of strangers disappeared with the last war. It is more difficult where the stranger happens to be of the opposite sex and where only two people are concerned.

Nevertheless, even in the best society, today, much can be done, provided it is nicely done, at the right time, in the right way and to the right person.

The middle-aged "married-looking" man who tries to "get off" with the attractive girl in the restaurant deserves what trouble he gets, if any. The young man, even were he simply to use the very suspect "Could you please tell me the correct time?" (suspect because it's as old as the hills as a method of trying to get acquainted) might get away with it, if the girl liked the look of him.

Far better methods can of course be thought out, depending on the situation. A kindly offer of a menu or cruet, an appropriate remark about an accident to crockery, or even a well-timed and skilfully executed lifting of the eyebrows as some odd-looking fellow diner leaves might (or might not) all serve as a means of introduction.

I remember some years ago a very attractive girl asked me the way to a station. I explained she could either go directly, which she would have to if she wanted her train, or in a roundabout way if she was content to catch the evening train. We had an enjoyable day. Where there's a will, as we say in Scotland, there's a way!

Difficult as is the meeting of strangers, even more difficult is the continuing of a conversation for many people after thay have been introduced. Introduction, after all, does not make a good companion. It certainly does not make a conversation. With people you don't know at all, conversation can be extremely trying unless you work to some sort of plan.

God preserve us from planned conversation and, in fact, most of this book is written just for that purpose— to show you how you can develop conversation which is enjoyable, interesting and spontaneous—how you can talk from the heart and mind.

All the same, the very shy and inexperienced will undoubtedly benefit if they can construct for themselves some sort of life-saving list of subjects to work on when the weather, the latest film and so on have served their purpose in the first few minutes. This list can largely be discarded when you have really become a conversationalist proper—but till then it can be useful.

1. *Humorous happenings to yourself.* People like to hear these and often help the conversation by telling their own.

2. *The Narrow Escape Story.* Here is another favourite. Most of us have had some exciting experience which for the story's sake we can perhaps slightly exaggerate, but be very careful how you go because in a company there is sometimes a stickler for hard facts who will pull you right up. I am reminded of the motorist who boasted of when he skidded and the car turned right round four times. I happened to know this is scientifically impossible but kept silent. After all, his story was good and told for our benefit.

3. *Funny stories.* As I explain later it is usually always best only to introduce subjects which are appropriate to the time, place and company, but in desperate silences desperate remedies can be tried . . . with care.

4. *Confidences.* In certain trusted company, personal experiences are not only permissible but acceptable. They form topics which can provide almost endless conversation, but of course you must remember the larger the company the greater the risk of the confidence not being respected. With two people the risk is less but nothing is secret which has been told!

5. *Character Reading.* This takes a lot of practice and experience but if skilfully done can provide great amusement. As with confidences care is required—remember the law of slander! And don't forget either that some

people are sensitive. In the right company fun may be had by all whether character is read from the lines of the face, the hands or tea-cups.

6. *Religion and Politics*. These are best left alone unless all the company are of the same creed.

7. *Health*. This can be boring especially if its about your own health, but if you can contribute something showing the courage of another it often makes a good topic.

8. *'Shop.'* Another subject which is apt to bore but like the weather is probably one of the most common subjects spoken about. Discussing your job, if it is interesting, can be a good topic.

9. *Holidays you've had*. Another subject normally overworked but if the holiday has involved travel there is lots of hope. It depends what you have seen and done and of course as most people go for holidays it is a fertile subject for others to contribute to.

10. *Families*. Parents find much in common in discussing children. In other family affairs much care is needed not to divulge family secrets but simple questions about the size of the family, where the different members live and the like do form ice-breaking topics. One point here is that it is not regarded as polite to ask a person what is their trade or profession.

11. *Hobbies, Sport, Pastimes*. These, of course, are good stand-bys provided a proper angle of approach is used. It is useless to talk the language of the rugger man to someone who never played the game. But often a lasting subject can be developed by, say, explaining the game to someone who has had sufficient interest to have watched it.

My message in this simple chapter is this. Like all the best things in life, it requires thought, much thought and more and more thought, before you become a worthwhile conversationalist and are regarded as "good company".

It is, of course, true that before a person can feel at ease with people he or she does require some knowledge of how the different sexes behave towards each other.

CHAPTER II

THE GOOD CONVERSATIONALIST

EACH one who wishes to be a good conversationalist has a clear mental picture of the kind of person he would like to be.

There he is, over among that crowd of people—this person we would like to be. He is the most important individual in the group, not because he is socially the most prominent, nor the most influential in business, nor the wealthiest, nor the most handsome in the gathering.

He is its most important member because without him conversation would end and the group would disperse.

He is vital because he is holding a number of people together in such a way that individuals are chatting happily to their neighbours. Were he to withdraw, the company would separate into knots of two or three people; there would be no general theme and some of them would begin to feel lost or bored.

Those of us who are interested in the art of conversation will find it profitable to study this man closely, to see what kind of man he is, no less than to observe exactly what he is doing and how he is doing it.

This examination is the purpose of our book. It is written in the conviction that most of us can succeed in conversation. Study of conversation, together with experience in teaching people how to develop fluency in both thought and speech—and that is the foundation on which the art of conversation rests—shows that success in conversation does not belong to people who have some facility of speech (amounting sometimes to glibness) joined to a superficial amiability. Much more surely it belongs to those who study the nature of conversation, see for themselves the principles underlying it and make themselves expert in the methods by which true conversation is promoted.

Now none of these requirements, neither the study nor the understanding nor the practice of the means of conversation, is beyond the grasp of any ordinary person.

With this in mind (and you may put a question mark after it for the moment, if you are doubtful about it) and before going on to consider this expert conversationalist who is our ideal—let us pause to note the differences between the ready talker and the man who can make conversation.

This book does not aim to help everyone to acquire only a smooth flow of words plus an assumed agreeableness of manner. In fact, verbal fluency plus an insincere geniality must be discarded by all who would make themselves proficient in the art of conversation. As you will see more clearly within a few pages, some of our best conversationalists were not always pleasant to their companions and, oddly enough, often spoke little.

IMPORTANCE OF LISTENING

This indicates a significant opening point, namely, whereas one might assume a book on conversation sets out to make you a good talker, it might more reasonably be said to help you to become a good listener! Whether speaking or listening is, on balance, the more important in conversation you will decide for yourself in due course. You will at least have no doubt that the silences of a conversationalist are as necessary to him as his ability to express himself clearly and interestingly.

With this brief introduction to what follows, examine

again the man whom we mentioned earlier, who was the centre of a lively conversation.

It will quickly become obvious that he is holding his group of friends together by keeping a firm grip on their interest. The men and women around him are not especially interested in him. At times, indeed, they may appear to have forgotten him. They are interested wholly in what they are discussing.

From time to time he says something which draws attention to himself or he tells an anecdote which makes the others laugh or which launches the conversation with fresh vigour and possibly in a new direction—perhaps five or even ten minutes pass without his speaking again.

What, then, is he doing? Why is he important? In a sense, we shall spend much of this book in answering that.

Here, we are content to notice his activities. Occasionally, for instance, he may reply to something said to him—when he does so what he says is usually amusing or witty and frequently brief.

If he tells a story, we notice that he does not do so for the sake of the story. That is to say, his stories are not told for the purpose of entertainment. They always help forward the conversation, providing a new viewpoint, offering fresh evidence one way or another or perhaps changing the direction of the conversation.

Now he is expressing his own point of view about the subject being discussed. Next he turns to a companion to invite another opinion. Later, he may quote something he has heard or read. All the time, we observe, he is concentrating on one thing only . . . the interest of those around him. Seemingly without effort he is keeping that group of men and women interested, both in each other and in the topics of conversation which succeed each other without pause. These people are making conversation among themselves and enjoying it. It is his aim they should do so.

The secret is that he knows how to discover what these people like to talk about and how to ensure that they develop their subjects along lines of wide general interest. Because he knows those two things people say he is "good company". They like to be with him, to talk to each other when he is present because he always makes conversation easy and pleasant.

Now that we have noticed so much, we begin to understand why he is always successful in talking to people, whether socially among acquaintances or more intimately with his friends. His interest is in conversation as well as in people. In these two interests he is never insincere, never talkative. In fact, only a trained observer would be likely to notice how little he says but how suitable that little is for promoting fluency of conversation among those in whose company he happens to be. His gift is to pull people out of their shells.

We now come to our second main point. You may be inclined to say at this stage—"Well, I think that I realised all these facts before. My personal difficulty lies not so much in wondering what a good conversationalist is and what he does as in trying to discover how he does it. That is, how I may do the same things myself. To some extent I know what is wanted but I do not know how to supply it."

This is the start of our inquiry into the art of making conversation and friends. From here we must go, step by step and with patience and not assuming that any step can be omitted, through the principles and methods which are outlined.

BEGIN BY THINKING ABOUT INTEREST

If you doubt that this is the most fundamental part of a

conversation try the experiment of talking to a boy of twelve. There is only one way of making certain that he will talk back—that he will actually exchange ideas with you instead of merely giving monosyllabic answers to your questions. Talk to him about his stamp album or his bicycle—his pets or favourite sports. If you are not wise enough to base the conversation on something which interests him he will soon lapse into an unhappy silence.

This applies equally to talking with adults—*you must make interest the foundation of your exchange of ideas.* Now and again you may find that the other person is not interested in any of the things you mention. Not every woman wants to think or talk about the furniture in her home or her children; not every man is a keen gardener or football fan. Here as always the exception proves the rule, but it should not be too difficult to find out what other interests a person has and conversation will readily follow your discovering the lines along which the particular mind runs most easily.

If you once grasp the fact that conversation rests on interest, whether personal or social or professional, and that without interest there can be no sustained conversation, you accept the most important truth as to why and how people talk to each other.

Here is what one of the friends of that supremely good conversationalist, Dr. Samuel Johnson, wrote about him. "He encouraged others to speak, especially young men, and paid due attention to what they said."

This is an illuminating statement because it leads to another point we shall shortly make and because it corrects a misunderstanding about Johnson. He is believed by many to have been an incessant talker who expected others to listen to him while he discoursed on any subject. This is untrue. Johnson was capable of sustained speech as are all good conversationalists and in such a way that his listeners wanted to continue listening. He was a great and fascinating talker. But talking and conversation are different things—and what made Johnson outstanding was his excellence as a conversationalist. Before going further into this, we should look at that short quotation again, take it to pieces and notice all it tells us.

"*He encouraged others to speak.*" In other words he found out the things in which they were interested and helped them to talk about those things. Even a cursory reading of Boswell's famous *Life* will bear that out.

"*Especially young men.*" This is really an astonishing fact. Remember that Johnson was rightly reputed to be one of the most learned thinkers of his time. He was the kind of man in whose presence you or I would certainly be silent and self-conscious. Yet we are assured that he was so anxious for other people to do the talking, and to tell him their ideas, that he took special care to encourage young men to converse with him. That is, people who above all others might be expected to be diffident in his company. Young men, too, are inexperienced. They are usually not the best read nor the best informed people. If they are sensible, they realise that they are unable to meet older people equally in an exchange of mature and informed opinion. All too often they may have experienced among their seniors, usually not endowed with Johnson's knowledge or depth of thought, that irritable intolerance and "Don't talk nonsense, my dear fellow", which keeps so many people silent.

Far from being impatient with younger men, Johnson went to special exertions to draw them into talk, and when they began to speak to him he "*paid a due attention to what they said*".

A friend of Johnson, named Tyers, remarked that the doctor had this habit of drawing people into conversation in the same marked degree as the philosopher, his contemporary, John Locke. Tyers said that both men were accustomed to *"leading people to talk on their favourite subject, and on what they knew best"*.

In other words, both men were determined to learn the interests of other people and enable them to speak of those things.

Here is our first and most important lesson as we contemplate the successful conversationalist and examine what he is doing. For him conversation is not a means by which he can empty his mind of all that is in it but an art by which he can promote an exchange of ideas which is useful to all who are talking together.

Note well one implication in what we have discovered about Johnson and Locke and all true conversationalists— *that they appreciated the best qualities of those in their company.*

Keep this in mind, especially as we are at times aware that not every quality in the minds or characters of our friends or acquaintances can claim our admiration. When the traits which displease us are apparent it may be difficult for us not to express, or at least fail to conceal our reactions.

Indeed, Johnson sometimes handled his friends roughly. Many of his remarks to them were ill-mannered, ill-humoured, untimely and not infrequently devastatingly critical. One finds, however, that these exhibitions concern Johnson the man rather than the conversationalist; they were indulged when Johnson was being pestered by importunity or was in the mood for man-to-man argument rather than a genuine exchange of views. Even where we find the doctor meeting new acquaintances uncouthly (and his first meeting with Boswell is the classical example of his humorous boorishness) we notice that he soon sought opportunity to make them feel at their ease with him.

Most of us are at times guilty of impatience and hastiness. This is not inconsistent with a resolution to discover

the best qualities in the people we meet. And this resolution is essential to successful conversion for, while a
knowledge of the interests of others is the foundation on
which talking with them rests, it is not in itself sufficient
to make conversation all that it should be. Without a more
human element it will remain artificial and impersonal.
We must know and like something in people before we
can talk to them with sincere interest. There must be
sympathy—which does not necessarily imply agreement.
What is meant here by sympathy will become clear later.

APPRECIATING OTHERS

I believe that this was in Johnson's mind when, in the
course of one of their early meetings, he told Boswell that
he liked to engage young men in conversation because,
among other reasons, "*they have more generous sentiments in
every respect*". Their views might be ill-formed and im-
mature. Their judgments might be hastily formed.
Their statements might be too dogmatic and self-assured.
All these defects must have been irritating to Johnson,
but they did not make him impatient. In them he saw
only the eagerness of youth, zest for life, alertness of mind
and a will to join as men in the company of men. Instead of
"I'm old enough to be your father" his unspoken reaction
was "There is much to be said for being young."

We must try not only to know the interests of the people
we meet but to appreciate whatever is good about them;
even about the things which appear to us to be their
faults.

In his intercourse with the great orator, Edmund Burke,
Johnson came to the conclusion that Burke preferred
talking to listening. Once he complained, "*So desirous is he
to talk that if one is speaking at this end of the table he'll speak
to somebody at the other end.*" Annoying though this must
have been, he did not let it prevent his seeing the qualities

which made Burke eminent even in the excellent company to which both men were accustomed. Many times he acclaimed Burke as an excellent man with whom to hold conversation, praising his power of perpetual thought, referring to his great wisdom and pointing out his gift for making any subject interesting to his audience.

Rather curiously his complaint against Burke appears to have been ill-founded. It is interesting to note that often Burke was more anxious to be in Johnson's company than the doctor found convenient. After spending an evening at Johnson's he remarked to Bennet Langton "How very great Johnson has been tonight!" Langton agreed but wished that they had been able to enjoy more of Burke's own talking. "Oh, no," Burke answered heartily, "it is enough for me to have rung the bell to him."

Here we have an outstanding example of two conversationalists of exceptional talent, each eager to help the other to open out his views on matters which interested him and each eager to appreciate the best in the character of the other. This is in itself a lesson in the art of good conversation.

CHAPTER III

THE THOUGHT DRIFT

AFTER introducing the subject of conversation as an art it would be easy to continue by further consideration of the successful conversationalist. I could consider the qualifications of mind and heart which he enjoys, or some of his methods, such as his use of anecdote or repartee.

These subjects I postpone, however, for later chapters, since there will be readers who by now will say *"This is all very true, no doubt. But it does nothing more than hold before me a picture of what I want to be. The more I look at it, the more sure I am I shall never achieve it."*

Conquer your discouragement! It is based on diffidence, and, more dangerously, on a conviction that you are often at a loss "for something to talk about." It is my job to remove this fear.

Nine people out of ten who are hesitant about their ability in conversation suffer from the fear that they must fail because they "cannot think of anything to say" or don't know what to do with possible conversational topics.

Admittedly the main difficulty in opening a conversation is in knowing what to talk about. That is inevitable as our first job is to find and hold the other person's interest. If we don't know what interests him then we don't know what to talk about. Sometimes the difficulty is increased by the diffidence or conversational inexperience of our companion so that he cannot frame a reply which will promote conversation. He can neither seize the rope we fling him nor throw one to us to cover the gap between us.

FINDING A TOPIC FOR CONVERSATION—AUTOMATICALLY

Many people appear to resemble the unhappy man pictured in Dryden's lines:—

"He trudged along, unknowing what he sought,
And whistled as went, for want of thought."
                              (*Cymon and Iphigenia*, line 84).

I say they appear to resemble this man, for everyone has thoughts, ideas, opinions and wishes. Conversational difficulty arises because these men seem to dissolve into nothing when needed. In some, the mind becomes blank, the thoughts frozen—all through ignorance of the rules and consequent fear. Fluency of thought and expression is the answer to this most deadly evil. The methods outlined here are designed specially to enable you to attain both.

Far from finding that your thoughts no longer come easily, you will find that you can think without effort on eight or nine topics of conversation within a minute or two of needing them. You will discover that if you make the slight initial effort required to start the psychological process suggested your mind will not empty but will automatically fill up with ideas.

Notice that word *automatically*. In it lies the secret of fluency of thought. The method explained here works according to nature; it is not artificial but follows the laws governing the mental processes. Consequently as soon as the method is used the mind responds and ideas move about it abundantly. The psycho-analysts have used a similar treatment, known as "free-association". To understand why this is so and to feel assured that what you are reading is solid and helpful, consider for a minute or two how your mind works.

The thought now going into your mind is entering a room already fairly full of ideas, and it fits comfortably among the other thoughts present there. These thoughts are constantly changing. This morning, for instance, you received certain ideas while you were reading your morning newspaper, from conversations overheard while you travelled in the bus or train, from things which you saw in shop windows, in the office or at home. Most of these ideas have already left your mind. Where did they go?

At the same period during which these thoughts occupied your attention other thoughts came into your mind which certainly did not enter, like those of the first kinds, from the outside world. For example, when the bus back-fired, you thought of a rifle shot and afterwards of war, or of a murder which took place in the film you saw last night. Again, when you noticed a green hat in a shop, you thought quite automatically of a friend who has a similar hat.

These thoughts came from inside you. Where did they come from?

WHERE THOUGHTS ARISE

It is clear that your conscious mind, which is incessantly receiving thoughts both from within and without, has a much larger mind at the back of it, a subconscious mind which is like a room with walls capable of indefinite expansion. Its walls are able to be enlarged almost to an unlimited extent. Into this lumber room the conscious mind pushes every thought, impression or imagination for which the outside world and its activities are responsible.

Here in the store room everything is infallibly registered and fitted away. Even during hours of sleep enormous activity goes on in the subconscious mind. *We could call it the store-away mind.*

Realising this, people sometimes say, "I will sleep on it". It is a common experience for them to find on waking that their mind has formed an answer to their problem in the night. The ever active subconscious mind has worked on the problem while they slept.

Recognise that in this store room we have the experience of all our years to draw upon as topics. Thus we are not limited to the conventional and obvious weather, politics, health, hobbies and gardening. Any of these may provide a good source of conversation, of course, but I want to teach you how to have a wider choice than that.

CHOICE FROM THE STORE-AWAY MIND

You will now realise that the subconscious mind, without our being in any way aware of the process, is always preparing and storing subjects for conversation. Ideas which we have bundled into it have not only been sorted and stored, but fitted together and related. Fact has been linked to fact, thought to thought, by association of ideas, so that a sequence of thought is prepared. Because of this activity, conversation is at the first stage only the tapping of an inexhaustible spring. It's wonderful, isn't it? Tap the spring and the resources behind it flow out by their own abundant energy.

Apart from the comparatively slight initial effort needed to open the mind to receiving ideas the rest of the work consists of directing the energetic flow of thought which enters the active or conscious mind. If you wish you may call the method we are studying the tapping of the mind's resources.

To appreciate to the full the possibilities resulting from this simple act, think of the mind as an ocean and not as a spring. Your thoughts might be likened to fishes swimming there. They are of many species. Moreover, they move in shoals. In the same way your ideas are separate and distinct from each other, but they are sorted out and placed close to each other by the subconscious mind.

If you bring one idea to the surface of the mind, it will be followed by others which are drawn up with it by the lines of inter-relation existing between all ideas which can be associated with each other. If we like we may fish with a line or a net, either looking for a certain idea or for a shoal of similar ideas from which to choose precisely what is needed.

Here is the beginning of our method of acquiring thought fluency. That is why this chapter is entitled the Thought Drift.

As a start, we will be content to let the mind do its own drifting while we watch what happens.

The process is no more haphazard than deep sea fishing. To the uninformed observer, drifting appears a casual, happy-go-lucky affair. The man in charge of it, however, knows well that it is wholly purposeful and that nothing is left to chance.

MENTAL 'DRIFTING'

To start your own mental drifting, take a pencil and a sheet of paper. Look at one of the many objects around you at the moment . . . the *electric light bulb*, a *chair*, a *vase*.

Close your eyes for a moment and do not think.

Simply let your mind drift round one of these objects.

After a moment or two, note on your paper the ideas which came into your mind. It is not necessary to our purpose that you should write them in the order in which they came into your mind.

As we are going through this training together, let me show you what happens to me so that you will know you are doing what is required. I look at a *chair*; then I allow my thoughts to drift about it. My mind leaves the chair, but does not actually go astray. It thinks of wood. Wood means *forests* . . . peaceful, sunny days when I have holidayed in the pleasant countryside.

Automatically I think of the friend who shared those days with me. In imagination I see him, recall the kind of clothes he wore . . . perhaps a little out of date in style for today.

Well, there we can break off the line of thought which has, by the mind's own activity, been offered to me. Notice that I made no effort at all except that first slight one of focusing the mind on one object. The thoughts came much more quickly than one could write them down.

THOUGHTS COME QUICKLY

Now we look at these ideas separately. Chair—wood—forests—holidays—a friend—clothes—fashion. I wonder where it might have ended if it had been allowed to continue. As it is there are six possible subjects of conversation, excluding the chair with which we started. This is, of course, only the beginning of our method, merely an indication of the way in which you allow your mind to work for you.

A first step in finding "something to talk about" is to let your mind wander off on its own after you have given it a starting point (and what that point may be is entirely unimportant) so that it works its way naturally forward from something suggested to it by one of your senses. A sight, a sound, a smell, any sense perception is adequate for the beginning of our method.

The second step is to generalise the ideas so produced, if this is helpful. For instance, *my friend* would not be particularly interesting to anyone else as a conversational topic, so that idea I would generalise into *friendship* or *friends* or *goodwill*. It could be generalised and developed much further, of course, but we don't want to go too far afield at the beginning.

What happens in this second stage is still automatic. Just as your mind will draw one thought after another for you, in a sequence of ideas, so if stopped at any one of them it will spread all round it. Or, if you prefer the illustration, if stopped from moving in a vertical line of thought at one point, it will then proceed from that point towards all points of the compass. You can choose to follow it along any one of these developing lines of thought. Thus from the mental image of your friend, you might generalise the idea into friendship, and arrive at an idea about international goodwill. You halt at this point because it ties up with an incident in the newspaper which struck you as interesting or significant. Here is your precise subject for conversation.

You may want to rush ahead to see where we go from here. Do that if you wish, but it is better to learn step by step and not to proceed from one step to the next until you have considered and *practised* the point dealt with.

Before going further, and as a reassurance in case you have that "my mind goes blank" affliction, notice how easy and almost entirely effortless this method is. It doesn't mean that at the very beginning of a possible conversation you pass into a kind of starry-eyed trance, during which the other person decides to leave before you become dangerous! What you are reading now, and will shortly practise, actually happens in seconds. It will take less time to go through than you use to light a cigarette.

This is because it is entirely natural. It is the way in which your mind wants to work. If it is unfamiliar and now sounds strange to you, that is only because you have never analysed how conversations actually begin inside you.

CONVERSATION *IS* NATURAL

It is therefore in marked contrast with the feverish efforts which may people make in order to "get a conversation going". The harder they try to find "something to talk about" the more self-conscious they become, until they understand all the agonies of the goggle-eyed, semi-paralysed characters in whom P. G. Wodehouse so happily specialises. *Failure is chiefly due to the fact that efforts to think of something are blocking the efforts which their minds are making to suggest something.* GET THAT.

The secret of starting a conversation is to let your mind do the work for you. It will, always and unfailingly, if you give it the chance to do so. This method, of natural, effortless thinking is the opportunity it needs.

Now let us look at another thought sequence.

To let my mind begin the sequence I looked at a reading lamp on my desk. Here is the chain of ideas which automatically came to mind within a minute of my noticing the lamp and allowing my mind freedom to wander.

Lamp — Inventions — Cinema — Actors — History — Time—Purpose of Life—Family—Starvation—Disease —Science—and Goodwill. As a mere list of ideas it is more or less incomprehensible. Notice that this fact is unimportant, since we did not set out to find a sequence of thought but rather a number of conversational subjects. And here they are, all twelve of them.

How did the mind find them for itself. The *Lamp* recalled to me the *Invention* of the electric bulb, and I remembered an excellent film I once saw (*Cinema*) about the life of Edison. This brought to my mind certain screen *Actors* and with this recollection came to mind (I can't see the connection yet, but this is irrelevant to our purpose) a character part played by Sam Jaffe in a film about Catherine the Great.

Since *History* is one of my reading hobbies, the remembering of this film inevitably led my mind to history and so to the idea of the passage of time. Instantly I thought of the years that had gone and that were to come and my mind considered the *Purpose of Life*. This obviously in most men's hearts is the creation and bringing up of a *Family*.

In the international turmoil the first care of men and women is for the children, an idea which hardened into the more definite thought of the *Starvation* suffered by children in war-time. Hunger leads to *Disease*, so that medical *Science* is called on for help. Notice there, by the way, how my mind did not focus on the science of Medicine but on Science in general. Not a really logical thing for it to do and while I am writing this out I begin to understand why my own mind played this trick on me. The reasons are not worth a mention, but the fact that the mind picks and chooses like this for itself is certainly worth noting in relation to its ability to deal with the requirements of conversation. There is no danger, you see, that by using the method explained here your mind will become standardised or made to work according to a pattern. Every mind uses the method in its own way and with results different from those reached by others.

Finally came the brief reflection that while science cannot remove the causes of suffering due to war, *Goodwill* among men and nations can prevent what science can only repair. Or is this wholly true? What about science and goodwill joined and working together for peace?

Well, there is no need to follow that line of thought here but in the list of topics I have linked the two subjects as indicating a possible thirteenth to the list.

The purpose of this list is not to find a line of thought but a number of items. To try to use this line as the backbone of a conversation would be fatal to the interest of anyone with whom you might try to talk. For one thing, several items in it are probably dull except for the mind which thought of them. Even to this mind they were

c

attractive only because they occurred in certain associations of ideas.

No, our aim is not to inflict all these topics on someone nor to drag him through the whole line of thought which my mind only and on only this occasion joined together. *I have shown how to discover a number of conversational topics by the aid of which we may discover where another person's interests lie.* Once this has been found conversation becomes possible. We shall go into this more fully later.

For the moment we may be content to know that we have a method by which, after a slight initial effort, the mind automatically provides us with a variety of possible subjects. With the help of our Thought Drift we now have them present in the conscious mind. Aware of them and of the person to whom we are going to talk, we can select one topic which seems most likely to arouse his interest. If there is no useful response, we can fall back on another subject from our list.

How does all this work out in practice?

That, you will shortly find out here you should not try to form any opinion as to what is likely to happen, for two most important points must be considered before we can understand the value of this method.

The first is that at this stage we possess only an outline of conversational possibilities. This outline is in its most awkward form being only a succession of knots on an invisible thread. The diffident talker may, for instance, imagine himself with a mind charged with frighteningly unrelated ideas which he is to cast one after another at some casual acquaintance. The results would be disastrous.

In a later chapter I shall explain how these stark ideas can be transformed into conversational topics.

Remember that even while we try one topic or another in conversation, our companion's mind is also drifting to some purpose. Our mention of a subject should suffice to start him thinking. What you say should cause some re-actions in his mind, any one of which may serve to make this first beginning a good opening for an exchange of ideas.

OPENING A CONVERSATION

It is important to realise that when you select a topic of conversation you are not expected to deliver the whole of it as it is in your own mind. Conversation is easier than making speeches . . . *far easier*.

The shy person is apt to forget that he is speaking to another mind which normally responds to suggested ideas. It is usually this response, rather than your first proposal, which is the beginning of conversation. To illustrate, if I mention rheumatic twinges and have in mind a remedy which I consider useful, my friend may make ıch a reply that my cure may never be mentioned. .e may react by referring to his own treatment or by .ntroducing some furthcr topic of medical discovery, or he may even declare his emphatic conviction that rheumatism is a product of the imagination!

For the purpose of conversation it is unimportant what opinion he advances. What matters is that his interest has been aroused; the conversation launched. Your partner has revealed something of his own mind. *You are no longer dependent on your ideas* but can make use of those which your companion puts forward.

Before reading further practise the following:—

EXERCISE

1. Starting from some object perceived by your senses (a table, the perfume of flowers, music, the weight or smoothness of something you are handling, the flavour of a cigarette)—let your thoughts drift without any

attempt to guide them. Make a mental note of each idea which occurs to you.

2. If any item in your list is particular, such as a *garden*, make it general, i.e. *gardening* or *gardens*. This widens the scope, making it more suitable for conversation.

3. Use this method in talking to some friend with whom you feel at ease. If the first topic or two which you select from the list provided by your Thought Drift does not cause the desired response, you will thus not be specially upset and will find it easier to persist in proposing further subjects to discuss.

CHAPTER IV

GIVING IT DEPTH

FLUENCY of thought and speech is not the same as facility in thinking and speaking. What is fluent flows; what is facile slips easily along. Fluency has depth; facility is superficial. The mind talks; the tongue only speaks.

A superficial conversation passing lightly over a variety of topics without pausing long on any one of them is difficult to sustain.

The purpose of this chapter is to explain how thinness in conversation may be avoided. Even the lightest talking requires some depth of thought in order that it may interest.

Some suggested topic may not secure the interest we hoped. Suppose for example that a person has responded to the general subject of *plants*. This alone may be adequate to maintain a hold for a few minutes, but unless the subject is given depth the conversation resting on it must necessarily remain vague in its details. Probably this happens because, although the topic caught the other person's interest, it failed to secure that *kind* of interest in which he, perhaps, specialised. Too often a conversation ends abruptly only because its topic was presented head-on, so to speak. Try to raise subjects in such a way that they can be widened to enable people to speak about that part of the subject which interests them.

Realise that in order to talk about anything a man must make an effort—he must make known where his interest lies in the subject you have introduced in a general way. It is from this effort that the inexperienced or diffident person shrinks. He is unwilling to make known what the subject means to him, possibly out of shyness or because he assumes you to be more knowledgeable. Without the initial effort the conversation dies. Always play your part.

There are some subjects, for instance, *gardening*, about which people talk readily. It may be the expert guiding the novice or two enthusiasts discussing sweet-peas but such subjects are good because nobody is at all inhibited about them.

Apart from these few subjects, the conversationalist must make two moves before he can be reasonably sure of success. The first is to have ready a series of possible topics and we have considered the method of preparing them. The next move is to propose aspects of whichever of these topics appears to interest your audience. Success requires training and I shall try to outline a method which you can practise.

When you detect a response to the general topic you have introduced—while your friend or friends are discussing it in the usual conventional way—*your mind* should be dividing the topic into its categories.

This may sound formidable. It is, in fact, so simple that you can train yourself to do it automatically. A trained mind is so alert that the mention of a subject sets it off discovering a number of aspects within seconds.

Reflect on the topic already mentioned, *Plants*. As a conversational opening it has many possibilities but they may be lost unless we can instantly find where other people's interests rest. Are our companions interested in hot-house or open-air plants? Winter, Spring, Summer or Autumn growing? Or perennials? The cultivation of flowers for the table or of herbs? It will be a waste of time to discuss your ambition to grow the perfect rose if your friend is only interested in the destruction of fruit tree pests.

Cultivate the habit of classifying general topics. In this way you can discover which department or aspect is likely to be of use in any particular conversation.

To acquaint yourself with this, practise the following exercise.

EXERCISE

Take pencil and paper—write the word "Trees" at top centre. Now think. The subject is capable of divisions and sub-divisions as well as introducing a number of associated ideas. You may find your mind hurrying from one activity to another, dividing trees into hardwoods, conifers and so on, while at the same time thinking of the apple tree of "Linden Lea" or of the tree on which Judas hanged himself, perhaps not all of them as quickly as that. Yet in some instances, possibly, more ideas than those will arrive in that space of time. Continue thinking for a minute or two longer about the general subject, *Trees*. Jot down the ideas which occur to you until you have about a dozen.

Look at your notes. Sort out and classify the ideas. Note, and it is important to do so, that this is the stage at which you classify. *To do so sooner would be to disperse the flow of ideas.*

Later, you will find that you can separate ideas into categories or link them according to their affinities as they come to you. For now and until you have experience in allowing your mind to pick up ideas, wait before classifying.

When you have allocated your ideas you may find something like this:—

TREES

Trees in national symbolism (English Oak, Canadian Maple).
Famous old trees (The vine in Hampton Court).

Famous giant trees (such as the Californian redwoods).
Sayings connected with trees (Up a tree; You shall know a tree by its fruit).
The uses of different species of trees (from masts to pit-props and matches).
Popular beliefs about trees (the treacherous elm, etc.).
Nature's uses of trees (preventing soil erosion, etc.).

In making this list I have been playing the game with you. I have not spent more than a minute in letting the general subject drift in my mind but have done exactly what you did. I relaxed and allowed my mind to wander.

ANOTHER EXERCISE

Try one more exercise. This time it is slightly different and it takes us nearer the heart of the matter.

Take the word "Communications". Do not try to think quickly but allow your mind to freely associate with the word, considering it from all sides. Your purpose is to perceive the divisions into which the subject may be analysed.

When you believe you have compiled a reasonably complete list, mark it on your sheet of paper methodically. In the following summary of divisions, notice how each division is sub-divided. The analysis could have gone further, of course, but for the purpose of providing conversational topics it does not need to do so.

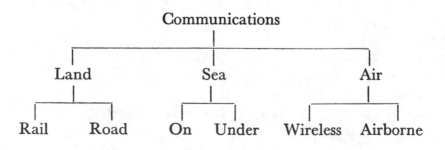

From here the mind advances quickly to divide under-sea communications into, for instance, marine cable and submarine transport. The idea "airborne" brings to mind air-mail, or air passengers or air transport of goods. There are also different kinds of aerial vehicle, rocket, combustion engine, jet. . . . A conversation might take wings with such a flow of subjects and lead away from "Communication" to supersonic speeds, physical science, peace, religion, and so on.

Our example shows how the method of deepening a general topic can assist a conversation to pass rapidly from its opening subject to others only remotely allied to it.

Remember, in talking to others, we do not try to conduct them along our own line of thought or force them to every apparent division of a subject. Our purpose is to discover a number of possible general topics and to deepen such of these as are of interest to our companions.

CHANGE AS YOU GO

Should your first choice of subject bring a poor response move on to another; if interest is shown, deepen the topic by mentioning one or more of its divisions. In the same way subdivide any division to which our companions react favourably.

This is but a stark theoretical outline—in practice it all becomes easier. Conversation is an exchange of ideas between two or more people. All the work is not left to one even though it may be that only one will know how to make good conversation possible. When he has succeeded in engaging the attention of another the latter begins to contribute his share. The responsibility is lifted. The opener's part changes. From being the soloist, he passes into the trio or quartet for the time being. Here he can be content to join in the talking, or, if he considers it wiser, allow the conversation to proceed without him, mindful of La Bruyere's observation "Conversation consists much less in showing a great deal of it than in causing others to discover it."

We all have memories of incidents which are interesting to other people. Let us use them in conversation. The result is increased interest and the conversation is both sustained and freshened because a personal angle has developed in it. It is like stepping off a high-road into an unexpected byway.

If you are aware of this small but important piece of technique you can gain pleasure and profit by watching it in use, apart from you own employment of it. Since it is natural, most people use it occasionally but without realising what they are doing. It is as natural to conversation as breathing is to the speaker and for this reason is all the easier to use simply and without being artificial.

In summary, what we have studied about the Thought Drift and how to develop it may be expressed in three words, Discover, Divide, and Spread. First find your topic, by having a series of subjects ready for use and introducing them until one of them strikes the spark of interest. Then divide the subject into its natural parts and spread the possibilities, occasionally at least, by introducing personal associations of ideas connected with the topic which has been established.

The following exercise, which introduces some minor means of development not found in the previous text, will be useful for practice.

ANOTHER EXERCISE

1. (a) List the topics derived from a Thought Drift starting from one of the following objects:—a cat; a dynamo; a statue; a musical chord; the colour red; a salad bowl; a horse; not being able to think of anything to say.

(b) Develop any topic obtained in this way dividing it into such parts as it seems to fall into naturally.

2. (a) Take any other topic from your list and connect some personal association with it, either to reveal it as it is in your own mind or to provide an opportunity for the conversation to pass from the topic to another.

(b) Do you know any anecdote which will illustrate any of the points which came into your mind while you were practising (a)? How would you relate the story?

3. Suppose that someone has tried to open a conversation with you by mentioning one of the following topics— Dentists — Games — News Bulletins — Hobbies — Reading—Cost of Living—Spring—Changing your Mind.

This is not an inspiring list, but gives you an excellent opportunity to practise making the conversation fresh and original. Let your mind drift round the topic you have selected and choose the most promising idea which occurs to you.

4. Take the topic, in the above list, which you like least and deal with it as in 2 (a).

CHAPTER V

BACKGROUND TO CONVERSATION

I HAVE endeavoured to answer the first of the two questions which arose at the beginning of the book—What shall I talk about? Now is the time to consider the answer to the further question—how shall I talk?

This involves the technique of continuing conversation with pleasure and profit when it has been established. You have learned how to start; learn now how to continue. Let us examine the main ornaments and personal qualities which elevate talking from a bare and dry exchange of ideas to a full communication of thought.

We shall study how to deal naturally and to easily convey the contents of our minds, all that has been stored by intelligence, memory, imagination, experience and sense of humour, to those among whom we talk. The art of concise self-expression demands an understanding not only of the subject matter but of methods of presenting it.

Sometimes we see the artistic method divided into the activities which are speculative and those which are practical. In literature, for instance, the speculative element consists of those activities which the author knows he wishes to communicate. The practical part of writing is made up of choice of form and the style to be used to get across to his readers exactly what he wants to put into their minds. In so far as he is able to choose the correct form, and to use that form successfully, the author is practical in his art. This is true whether he writes serious prose, fiction, allegory based on recognisable fact, verse or any other form. He must choose the right medium and the right technique for employing it. If he chooses to express himself in verse, he must know what verse demands of him and be able to supply the demand.

The art of conversation is less complicated but it has its own methods, which are chiefly psychological. We must know, in the practical side of this art, just how to say any given thing to a given person. Further we must know what means will fill that all-important "how".

In approaching the problems involved, we should not regard the qualifications of the conversationalist as so many artificial acquirements which he attaches to himself. They are not like pins in a pin-cushion. By constant practice the technique of good conversation must become part of him. An easy and natural employment of it will never be attained as long as we regard it as an instrument, something outside ourselves. Everything to do with conversation must be regarded as part of ourselves, completely identified with us. In brief, the points we are going to consider should form within us what we may call the "conversational personality". So natural may the art of conversation become, spontaneous and individual in each of us, that the poet Cowper, who rejoiced in it, could write;

> "Conversation in its better part
> May be esteemed a gift, and not an art."
> *(Conversation, I. 3)*

As a beginning, we may take up a point referred to in Chapter II, and remind ourselves that the conversationalist should:—

ALWAYS BE A GOOD LISTENER

In the twenty-fifth chapter of the first book of his *Essais*, Montaigne observes reflectively, "Silence and self-effacement are most valuable qualities in conversation". This truth is proverbial. The German has it that he cannot speak well who cannot hold his tongue, while the Italian, more briefly, says that the talkers sow and the silent reap. I must devote some space to a part of conversation which is of great importance.

This may not be appreciated by those who only ask that others should listen to their endless monologues. Such people are talkers and not conversationalists. The good conversationalist must learn when to speak and when to be silent.

Think again of the man whom we watched in Chapter II —the ideal conversationalist who controlled a discussion both by his silences and his timely interventions. He is no creature of the imagination for his counterpart is to be found among the great conversationalists of whom we have record.

An understanding of what he is doing shows us that the art of listening must be acquired and sincere and not merely assumed. To listen is an instinct which we must develop. Unless it becomes an acquired habit it will quickly forsake us so that we do not possess a trained ability in conversation.

This is so real a truth that a German proverb comments, "Education begins a gentleman, conversation completes him". That is, conversation consists of proper reticence as well as of suitable speech.

Good listening does not mean prolonged silence. To say nothing, to contribute nothing to what is said, is of little benefit to you or others. The silence of good listening, however, is attentive. It is a sympathetic silence, in the sense that it offers, in the true meaning of the word, the sympathy of your attention even when you disagree. Notice this fact, for you will soon perceive that you cannot extend this sympathetic listening to anyone without his coming to realise that you are anxious to hear him. Your attitude as a conversationalist will become apparent to him, without your saying or doing anything to reveal it, by a dozen details of your appearance and behaviour of which you may be unaware. How you look at him, the inclination of your head, the expressions which flit across your face, the unpremeditated movements of your hands, all convey close attention.

The impression he receives encourages him to express himself (even though he knows you disagree with his views). In this way you are helping the conversation.

The graces of conversation, the qualities which make it thrilling and delightful, require that you make this attentiveness a part of yourself and never a polite attitude.

GENUINE LISTENING VITAL

Genuinely attentive listening tells your companion that you consider he is worth your regard. It gives him confidence to continue with what he wishes to say. He takes special care to express himself as clearly as he can; he does not hesitate to correct himself; he feels encouraged to venture on an anecdote or comparison which will help his meaning. Your listening is promoting conversation more successfully than any series of comments or interruptions could do.

We have all at some time been compelled to talk to people who interrupted us by a series of interjections, remarks, questions or statements. Sometimes what was said contributed to the subject but often the addition was merely useless. It snapped our thought line, deflected us from our purpose and destroyed the pattern of our words. This illustrates the damage inexperienced or unkind listening can do.

Consider the personal advantages which the habit of sympathetic listening brings to our conversation.

It covers our weaknesses.

None have the ability to talk at large and on many occasions through the day without the risk of falling into faults which will spoil good conversation. If we do more talking than listening, we are likely to make mistakes in what we say or how we say it. We may easily become excited or confused. We may repeat ourselves or tell our anecdotes again in different conversations with the same person. The substance of our remarks will inevitably grow thinner and our jokes become familiar. We may become known as trying people to talk to or perhaps bores.

The discretion of silence saves us from these faults, which are as quickly noticed by others as they are harmful to us.

While we are not talking we can think. We have opportunity to consider what others are saying and to prepare our replies. *We can also make sure of the reasonableness of what we intend to say,* revise our method of expressing it *and watch for the right moment to do so.* It is good advice to "think twice before you speak once".

During periods of listening companions can be weighed up. You can come to know more of their interests so that when your turn comes to speak you can select appealing subjects.

While we listen, we watch. We note changes of expression. We gain an insight into the workings of other minds. We study traits of character as they reveal themselves. We think about what we see as well as of what is said.

The more accurately we observe others the easier it is for us to maintain conversation with them.

The knowledge thus acquired gives us an unobtrusive mastery over the conversation. We can lead it wherever we may wish among the interests of those about us.

This point shows clearly how the great conversationalists used the discipline of silence and attentive listening to gain ascendancy. The minds they addressed themselves to were as familiar to them as favourite volumes in their own libraries. Much practice in this discipline gave them the ability to penetrate and readily understand new acquaintances, so that presently their ability to succeed in any company was assured.

We may pass to another advantage of listening. Good listening adds emphasis to what we say. A mountain above a valley is more impressive than one rising from a plain. The occasional remark is often more effective than a continuing flow of talk.

This is not because what you say is an interruption nor because people feel obliged to listen to someone who has not taken a very active part. Rather it is because what you say is well thought out in advance.

Your interval of silence has, for instance, allowed you to recall the apt quotation which will illustrate your view better than you could in your own words.

YOU CAN QUOTE OTHERS

Perhaps you can now quote statistics or some authority in your support; it may be that you have recalled a story which will draw attention to the point you wish to make or enable your companions thus to see it from a clearly defined angle. The discipline of silence has kept you collected and resourceful so that what you say is the more welcome, because it is suitably expressed. *The easiest and best conversation is when a man has something to say.*

The emphasis which periods of silence give to your conversation is also due to the fact that you have been able to observe the effect which the conversation is having on those taking part in it. You realise, let us assume, that someone must be interrupted and another person drawn

D

in. You notice, too, the trend of the conversation and have time to consider whether it should be given a new direction or a fresh impulse to sustain it along its settled course. And this should be carefully noted, for too few people are aware of the shape and direction of a conversation. It moves along from idea to idea, losing itself, twisting back upon itself, splitting into various points not clearly noted as distinct from each other, and no one takes the trouble to keep it in hand. This happens because too many are talking and too few listening.

The silences of intelligent conversation are of great value to those who wish to be at their best in any verbal exchange of ideas. For them there is not that danger of which Montesquieu warned when he complained that he often lost an idea before he could think of words with which to clothe it. Instead of being so exposed to ment. isolation, they, by timely silences, are fluent in words and ready in thought, for they think all the time-both their own thoughts and consider what is being said. They are thus at the heart of the discussion and know well what Hazlitt meant when he commented, "The soul of conversation is sympathy."

Let us conclude this point by quotations from this writer who knew, especially in the circle round Charles and Mary Lamb, the art and pleasures of conversation at its best. In writing of *The Conversation of Authors* he gives a brief sketch of the good conversationalist and every word is worth study.

"The art of conversation is the art of hearing as well as of being heard. Authors in general are not good listeners. Some of the best talkers are, on this account, the worst company; and some who are very indifferent, but very great talkers, are as bad. It is sometimes wonderful to see how a person, who has been entertaining or tiring a company by the hour together, drops his countenance as if he had been shot, or had been seized with a sudden lockjaw, the moment anyone interposes a single observation. The best converser I know is, however, the best listener. I mean Mr. Northcote the painter. Painters by their profession are not bound to shine in conversation, and they shine the more. He lends his ear to an observation as if you had brought him a piece of news, and enters into it with as much avidity as if it interested himself personally."

Hazlitt now particularizes his general statement, and we may notice the various other advantages which he remarked in Northcote's conversation, and see how, in the light of what has been written here, their origin can be traced to his habit of punctuating conversation with silent periods of listening and preparation.

"If he repeats an old remark or story, it is with the same freshness and point as for the first time. It always arises out of the occasion, and has the stamp of originality. There is no parroting of himself. His look is a continual, every-varying history piece of what passes in his mind. His face is a book. There need be no marks of interjection or interrogation to what he says. His manner is quite picturesque. There is an excess of character and *naïvete* that never tires. His thoughts bubble and sparkle like beads on old wine. The fund of anecdote, the collection of curious particulars, is enough to set up any common retailer of jests that dines out every day; but these are not strung together like a row of galley-slaves, but are always introduced to illustrate some argument or bring out some fine distinction of character."

The last point in this list of details, the proper use of anecdote or illustration, we shall deal with fully later. In the meantime we recognize the portrait of a lively and interesting conversationalist.

Now we must leave our first rule, about sympathetic listening, to consider a second principle which must be observed during conversation.

TRY TO AVOID TELLING A MAN HE IS WRONG

You may imagine this is a foolish rule for to keep it would make conversation artificial. Yet the rule is an ancient one for all who speak in public, whether before a large audience or more privately with friends and life is always the happier and more successful because of it. This will be realized when we understand what it implies and this may be succinctly stated under two headings.

(a) If a man is at fault in a statement or an opinion and you must tell him so, set about the task in a way which will allow him to think or feel that the correction comes, at least in part, from himself. In real life conversation does not always flow with the academic smoothness of a discussion between Socrates and his friends. *People have feelings as well as thoughts*, and even though they wish to be reasonable they may still give way to unreason in their statements, solely because their feelings have been roused. Remembering that the aim of the conversationalist is to promote a continuing exchange of ideas, one would not say, "Rubbish! Utter nonsense!" in reply to a carefully stated expression of opinion. To do so would be to annoy, and the irritation would not be unreasonable. It would prompt the speaker to a hasty retort, possibly to a passionate or obstinate assertion of a view which he may himself begin to see is not entirely accurate.

Even if the incident is hurried over a damaging blow has been struck at the conversation in progress. How much wiser it is to insinuate the correction or disagreement, gently! A slowing up of speech, a delaying of the *tempo* of the conversation, may also be managed, so as to give the other man a chance to listen carefully to the way in which you differ from him. Try to make your own viewpoint fasten on to something he has said with which you agree; take a principle mutually accepted and reason from that to your own suggestions; take one of your friend's statements and show that it logically leads to your own idea rather than his. These are ways in which you can help your companion to change his view without having to say outright, "I was entirely wrong." Face-saving, if you like, but usually the best way.

(*b*) If this cannot be achieved, at least leave him some way of escape. We have all at times had to admit that we made a mistake in what we said, were in error as to fact, or were unreasonable. And most of us know what an unpleasant experience it is, when faced with someone without tact or human understanding, to have to climb down every rung of the ladder. Most of us can manage to climb down if we have to in honesty, but we don't care to be made to break our necks in doing so. Rather than do that, we may easily yield to the temptation to resist admitting that we were wrong. Profiting by this experience we may learn to make it as easy as possible for the other man to change his ideas without appearing to have been entirely wrong.

If you are still unconvinced of the value of this rule, which no writer of any authority has ever challenged, take it on faith for a time and practise it. You will discover its usefulness.

At this stage we may bring in another rule, since we are already on the fringes of disagreement in conversation. We should therefore be sure what our attitude to argument ought to be. An argument is often a healthy and enjoyable

activity especially where it is sweetened by wit and anecdote. But generally it is to be avoided in conversation.
Admitting that there are exceptional occasions, we must
nevertheless make it a rule that we:—

TRY NOT TO ARGUE

Experience is worth pages of instruction and in this
matter any thoughtful observance of what happens to
conversation when argument takes possession will make it
unnecessary for us to prove the value of the rule.

You will have noticed how passion rises, conviction is
hurled against conviction, exasperation grows and spreads
through most of the company while dangerous sarcasm
may be introduced. There is a time and a place for
argument, but it is not in conversation, which it ruins.

The rule is so obviously proper that we will spend our
time in considering how to observe it and not in proving
its worth. The following points are suggested.

(a) Try to see the other man's point of view. Try to
understand his reasons for holding it. As far as may be
possible to you, look at it in his way, through his mind,
and thus you will understand the view better in itself.
And you will be helped when your turn comes to put a
different opinion before him. If you can see his view as
he sees it, you have a better chance of securing his
genuine attention to your criticism of it. Your friend
should be assured that you have tried to understand him
and he will make an equal effort to give sympathetic
attention to what you say.

(b) Tell him what you accept from his statements, what
you admire in his opinions or his marshalling of facts. For
instance, you may comment on the good sense and logic
by which he has arrived at his conclusion, pointing out
your disagreement is with the principle or fact from
which he started his line of thought.

(*c*) Be endlessly patient. Keep your emotions and impulses firmly under control. In saying this, I am not one of those who believe that it takes two to make a quarrel, for some people are so argumentative and awkward especially if they are opinionated or inclined to mental snobbery, that it is almost impossible to avoid argument with them. At the same time we know that an argument, which has any other possible end except an agreement to differ, is useless to conversation. You may need endless patience, and the firmer you are in your own view the more patience you must possess.

(*d*) Always admit your mistakes readily. It is surely needless to write much about this point, especially in view of what has already been considered. We may add, however, that a willingness to admit any error as soon as you see it goes a long way towards establishing the goodwill necessary to profitable conversation. A grudging or partial admission of error causes obstacles which should never arise in the communication of ideas and opinions.

On occasions you will find yourself talking to people who are far from argumentative—the diffident, hesitant people who, even when they wish to join in conversation, hold back from doing so. In their company one should remember our next rule, which is that one should

BE ALIVE, AND EVEN CHALLENGING.

This means principally that one should be alert in manner. A smile is more inspiring than much persuasion. A cheerful face is always a good thing to see and many people have anxious or sad faces without yours being added to the number. A friendly and pleasant approach is more likely to draw people out of themselves than a sober formality.

But do not assume a hearty and forced cheerfulness that is so easily detected for the false thing it is. Anyone who is sensitive shrinks from it and distrusts those in whom they find it. Instead of this, be as cheerful as you can so as to convey to others a sense of ease and well-being. This is in itself encouraging. Those who know that you can brighten a few minutes will always be glad to listen to you and respond.

If you happen to suffer from diffidence in meeting people, remember that your attitude has a discouraging effect on them. You damp down the conversation before it has a chance to start. Sometimes people who feel uncomfortable with new acquaintances incline to hide their fault by blaming others and finding in them various reasons for their own discomfort. These reasons may exist but one should be honest enough to see if the fault is on one's own side. Even if you freeze up and can't think what to say at first, try to show a pleasant aspect to others and not a half-sulky appearance which may be understandable but is unhelpful and, most of all, unhelpful to yourself.

On both sides there should be a quiet but cheerful approach. This is less difficult to establish than many suppose.

Finally we come to a rule which is almost offensively obvious, yet often ignored.

KNOW WHAT YOU ARE TALKING ABOUT

We may as well deal first with the unmistakable meaning of the rule—that we should be sure of our facts and be modest in our opinions.

I remember recently listening to a man holding forth about a book which is well known among our classics but not widely read except among specialists in the particular subject. It happened that I knew the book and did not agree with his view of it, which appeared to me to be superficial. In the group was a man whom I knew to be more able to form a literary judgment than myself, being more widely read and having, I think, a sounder literary knowledge. So I held my peace. He did the same. After the speaker had left us, one of the guests asked this man, "Why didn't you say something? Perhaps because you agreed with everything said."

"He was too wrong for anyone to discuss the book with him," was the reply. "I didn't think it possible for a man to read the book and be so completely mistaken about it." Then he went on to express a different view of the book, leaving us with an awful sense of X's incompetence. X had even mixed the chapters and incidents, and had introduced one character from a book by a different author.

This illustration is in a sense trivial. But the effect of the incident on X was far from slight, for, if he had invited our confidence in his judgment in any matter at all, even about his own business which was eminently successful, he would have started at a disadvantage. Each of us had lost confidence in his thoroughness of examination, his powers of analysis, his memory, and his general reliability. A man who can be really inaccurate in one matter is often not supposed to be dependable in any.

Inaccuracy as to fact or looseness in thinking can do your conversation harm, if only because it damages the confidence which must exist between people who talk together. *In any conversation you must know what you are talking about.* If you feel ill-informed or if you know nothing of the topic being discussed, say so frankly. That will gain confidence and it will sustain your own confidence. No thinking person distrusts those who admit lack of information, for they can learn; none distrust the man who says he has not thought much about what is proposed, for he shows honesty.

These are our rules for successful conversation. In

discussing them we have perhaps given the impression that conversation is a sober business. It may have appeared to be a deadly serious exchange of opinions. Such an impression is misleading and we shall proceed at once to examine some of the ornaments which lighten the art of talking well amongst ourselves. An interchange of ideas, however serious it may be, can be whipped up by epigram and quotations, illuminated by anecdote, salted and sharpened by wit. You can express theories or say what your guess would be, so long as you make it clear you are doing only that.

Without ignoring them, except for the time being, it seemed wise in this one chapter to concentrate on the five rules which underlie all other parts of conversation.

If I were asked which of the rules is the most essential I would return to the first one, in the spirit of the proverb that conversation can teach more than meditation. In the simple statement of Montaigne, in the first book of his *Essais*, "Silence and self-effacement are more valuable qualities in conversation."

CHAPTER VI

REPARTEE

TURN now from the dry bones of our subject to consider some of the ornaments by which conversation is made outwardly attractive by examining facility in repartee or witty retort. Here, some readers, especially those most appreciative of good conversation, may feel like parting company, protesting that to analyse anything witty is also to damage it. They may feel that to try and cultivate in anyone the quality of saltiness or droll fancy is almost unnatural and destined to failure. For impromptu, as Molière observed, is the touchstone of wit.

This chapter begins under the handicap of these reflections. I believe, however, that with patience the reader will discover that some practical hints can be given. I am not writing about wit itself but confining myself to that part of it called repratee. Repartee is invariably an answer which (in forms which vary but are unexpected and humorous) ingeniously combines or contrasts elements of what has been said. By doing this, the reply checks or closes, advances or opens the topic involved.

For example, you may have heard the answer given to the lady who exclaimed, "Look at that snowflower braving all this bitter weather! What a plucky little flower!" To which was replied, "Well, there are braver flowers . . . think of those which face the English summer."

It is not easy to see exactly what that answer does. It is not merely cynical. Probably its best function is to lighten the conversation, to set gently aside a mild attack of "gush". Notice that it takes the statement and, by presenting it from a surprising and original angle, sends it back. In this instance, the reply does it in a form which leaves little opportunity for the speaker to make any further use of the topic; it closes the subject.

As another example there was the agitator who said to the farmer, "I am determined to get the agricultural worker an eight-hour day." The farmer replied, "Well, for myself, I'd be glad to get an eight-hour night!"

This takes us a step further in our analysis, for it does more than send the topic back to the speaker in a new form . . . in this case, it promotes the conversation by neatly expressing the fact that there is more than one point of view to be considered. You will notice that the method used is that of Contrast. *Night* is opposed to *day*, thereby implicitly contrasting the labourer's long day with the farmer's short night; the hard work of the one but the more prolonged work of the other.

Here then is one source of repartee. By considering the conversation of others and by reviewing your own contributions you can compare what was actually said with what might have been said had Contrast been used to enliven and illuminate. In reading, especially good fiction, make a mental note of the methods used wherever you find good repartee. Space prevents the lengthy quotation which would be needed to illustrate this here but that is no loss for it is far more useful for you to find your own examples. In reading P. G. Wodehouse, for example, do not be content to laugh at what is witty but pause to see why it is witty; to notice exactly how the author achieves his effect.

USE OF CONTRAST

Contrast of ideas is a common source of repartee and association of ideas is equally fruitful. Here by way of an aside we may slip in some recognition of the fact that Similarity of Sound can give rise to the salted reply, while not degenerating into a pun. For example, I once heard a man cough diplomatically after a remark by a friend of his in a mixed company. His friend glanced at him, half surprised and half amused at the hint, and asked, "I didn't say anything untowards, did I?" The answer was "No, I don't think so. But it was getting on towards, you know."

The sound of the question was like a pebble dropped into a pond. It set up ripples of association which spread in the mind of the listener until the sound of *untowards* suggested the form of his answer, that what had been said *was getting on towards what might be considered untowards.*

That point we notice merely in passing, for our chief concern is with Association of Ideas rather than of sounds. Recall the reply to the aphorism that "The perfect host is one who makes his guests feel at home." To which the experienced host replied, "Yes, even when he wishes they were." Here the association lies in the words *at home,* calling into mind that place in which we have at times heartily wished some long tarrying friend whom we nevertheless wanted to treat with kindliness. The words *at home,* linked with the idea of *perfect host,* showed the speaker that the form of his answer would give effectiveness to his idea and yet, by adding to it a humorous twist, rob it of sourness. Hence the success of the remark.

We come close to bruising the butterfly's wings in examining them but it must be done for our aim is to see how repartee arises and by so doing increase our use of it. Our studies may also save us from attempting what is imperfectly understood. Misunderstanding this kind of retort people sometimes allow themselves to make rude or cutting remarks thinking they are achieving minor brilliance in conversation.

Next consider a third method of repartee—division of what is said. For the sake of brevity, let us take a quotation from Wilde's *The Importance of being Earnest*, since it is really an aphorism plus repartee.

> "All women become like their mothers. That is their tragedy.
> No man does. That is his."

The reply is based not so much on Constrast between *man* and *woman* as between the fact that *woman* is only half of the race. If someone makes the statement about woman which Wilde wrote in that play, there is an almost instinctive urge to reply by completing the subject, through the addition of *man*. From here it is another step to framing the manner of the reply by affirming the opposite of what was said of woman. The thing is, in a sense, the outcome of an automatic habit of mind. In so far as the habit may become almost automatic, it is bad; yet because it does occasionally reveal the right form for a suitable answer, it is useful to practise.

The example given is, however, exceptional because the subject introduced (*woman*) is seen as one half of the whole (*race*). In most repartee arising from Division, the subject is seen as a whole, and the repartee starts because someone divides the subject. Perhaps one might say that Division of this kind is the source of most repartee.

This may be illustrated by the story of two Edinburgh ministers of bygone days, who took it in turn to preach the Sunday evening addresses. One extremely inclement winter evening, Samuel read prayers and returned to the vestry to find James discarding extremely wet clothing preparatory to donning his surplice. "I'm wet through to the skin," James moaned. "I'll catch my death of cold while I'm preaching!" "Never fear, James," remarked Samuel. "You'll be dry enough when you're in the pulpit."

This might be mistaken for repartee based on contrast whereas in fact Samuel split the second half of James's remark (about preaching) and applied the result to the first half (about being soaked through). You will find that this formula is frequently discernible in any crossfire of repartee you may read or hear. Another example may be found in a remark I once heard, made by a man who had a reputation for telling lengthy anecdotes. His answer showed that he had a ready wit which, to my own pleasure, successfully launched him into his story.

> "I'll tell you a story about that. A particularly good one, as it happens."
> "Oh, heavens, not another, old man. Frankly, your stories never seem to have any end."
> "No? Well this one is so exceptionally good that you'll find it hasn't even a beginning."

Other examples:—

> "Why do you ask so many indiscreet questions?"
> "But I don't. It's your answers which are indiscreet."

> "My husband is always trying."
> "All husbands are."
>
> (WILDE—*The Ideal Husband*)

Do you not now agree that repartee appears to be less spontaneous than we thought it was at the opening of this chapter?

Facility in quick and witty retort may be developed and there is no need to prove that statement since every power of the mind may be strengthened and trained. Not only can the mind develop its natural powers of rapid reply but it can learn how to apply these powers so that they may be useful. This may seem to some to be incredible and to others unorthodox. To anticipate the objection, that it makes conversation artificial or standardised— it must be admitted that knowledge of the right methods does not always produce the desired results.

Let us further consider the matter by quoting the proverb that "after-wit is everybody's wit", which is too often supposed to mean "fool's wit". The proverb recognises that, reflecting over a previous conversation, one often sees too late the witty answer which could have been given—if it had been thought of in time. This experience is depressing: for many is an almost insuperable stumbling block in their progress towards conversational success. Such discouragement is mistaken. This is seen if you realise that what is perceived too late is also perceived early.

That is, what is too late for one conversation is in hand for another. If some appropriate remark is useless for the conversation of an hour ago, it follows that it will be on the tip of your tongue when a similar opportunity occurs.

This is as far as I wish to take the point at the moment, for I shall be dealing with it again later. For now I am content to explode the idea that repartee must be spontaneous *at the moment it is uttered*. In some speakers it is instantaneous but they are experienced conversationalists. A similar gift may be developed by others, especially if they realise that most quick replies are merely the surface action of a mind which has thought deeply, worked out replies and trained itself.

You train your mind, as most of us can do, in the use of those methods and their use becomes spontaneous. It is important that you should know this.

WORK WILL GET RESULTS

It is a fact, just as it is a fact that skill in the use of anecdote, together with what seems to be an inexhaustible fund of stories, frequently derives from practice *plus a handy notebook which is perused before conversation.* There is nothing artificial about this. It is only adequate preparation. Who would expect an extempore lecturer to speak without the previous ordering of his thoughts and a checking over of his data? Who would expect a vocalist to sing without rehearsal which is, indeed, his constant occupation? And who will be so foolish as to expect success in conversation without a similar and proper preparation. It is worth the effort.

Thus it is not only correct to foresee, as often as possible, the remarks you may expect from among friends but also to note, mentally or in a book, those suitable replies which occurred to you too late against the occasion when they will be appropriate and, because they are in hand, immediate.

In case this view has destroyed any illusion and such an illusion will be even more dissipated presently, pause for a moment to ask yourself whether it makes the least difference to a conversation if the brilliant reply was spontaneous or whether it was part of the speaker's stock-in-trade? Its effect is the same. Then why should anyone be disappointed to think that not all repartee is the immediate scintillation of a brilliant mind?

It is understandable to feel, "How I wish I could sparkle and shine in conversation! How delightful it would be if witty remarks were to rise as rapidly in my mind as bubbles in a brook!"

Such an experience would be delightful. It would also be exceptional to the way the human mind works. If your companion tosses ideas about lightly and amusingly, be assured that he has (probably with tremendous labour)

E

done much thinking and paid attention to the art of expressing himself. His success lies in the fact that he can quickly find and group a variety of ideas, illustrations, anecdotes, quotations and authorities and express them entertainingly. However spontaneous much of his talk may be its origin is not spontaneous.

There is a passage in Hazlitt's essay *On the Difference between Writing and Speaking* worth considering, if only because his several statements combine to form a point, towards the conclusion, which I find is usually missed by readers.

This point is that while there is a comparative difference between people in that some think and speak or write more quickly than others, there is in effect little difference in their work. If Hazlitt were writing on the point we are considering, he would undoubtedly express the same point of view—that as far as conversation is concerned, it does not matter whether what you say by way of quick and effective reply is the result of preparation or of the inspiration of the moment. Here are his words:—

"The great leading distinction between writing and speaking is, that more time is allowed for the one than the other: and hence different faculties are required for, and different objects attained by, each. He is properly the best speaker who can collect together the greatest number of apposite ideas at a moment's warning: he is properly the best writer who can give utterance to the greatest quantity of valuable knowledge in the course of his whole life. The chief requisite for the one, then, appears to be a quickness and facility of perception—for the other, patience of soul, and a power increasing with the difficulties it has to master. He cannot be denied to be an expert speaker, a lively companion, who is never at a loss for something to

say on every occasion or subject that offers; he, by the
same rule, will make a respectable writer who, by dint
of study, can find out anything good to say upon one
point that has not been touched upon before, or who,
by asking for time, can give the most complete and
comprehensive view of any question. The one must be
done off-hand, at a single blow: the other can only be
done by a repetition of blows, by having time to think
and do better. In speaking, less is required of you, if
you only do it at once, with grace and spirit: in writing,
you stipulate for all that you are capable of, but you
have the choice of your own time and subject. You do
not expect from the manufacturer the same dispatch in
executing an order that you do from the shopkeeper or
warehouseman. The difference of *quicker* and *slower*
however, is not all: that is merely a difference of comparison in doing the same thing. . . ."

Hazlitt writes as if the gathering of many ideas at a
moment's warning, or the producing of one's effect off-
hand and at a single blow, is all instantaneous work
because it is immediate in effect. He would be horrified to
be understood in this sense, however, for he well knew,
being himself a distinguished conversationalist with a
keen interest in his art, that what is apparently instantaneous is often the result of long preparation. For this
reason he contemptuously sketches the man whose interest
is rather in the exhibition of his own brilliance, as he
supposes, than in the studied promotion of good talking
together. He has no use for those "whose chief ambition
is to shine by producing an immediate effect." Such
people are represented in his mind by . . .

"There is F——; meet him where you will in the
street, he has his topic ready to discharge in the same

breath with the customary form of salutation; he is hand in glove with it; on it goes and off, and he manages it like Wart his caliver . . . but, ere you have time to answer him, he is off like a shot, to repeat the same rounded, fluent observations, to others—a perfect master of the sentences, a walking polemic wound up for the day, a smartly bound political pocket book. . . . What does all this bustle, animation, plausibility, and command of words amount to? A lively flow of animal spirits, a good deal of confidence, a communicative turn, and a tolerably tenacious memory with respect to floating opinions and current phrases. Beyond the routine of the daily newspapers and coffee-house criticism, such persons do not venture to think at all: or if they did, it would be so much the worse for them, for they would only be perplexed in the attempt, and would perform their part in the mechanism of society with so much the less alacrity and easy volubility."

Further on in his essay Hazlitt is more indignant but it is not necessary to follow him since our point is now clear. Everyone may develop his powers of conversation by a study of the right methods and a careful practice of them.

EXTENDING A CONVERSATION

Let us turn to another type of repartee, which is when one takes what has been said further than the speaker intended or foresaw. This has been called the method of Exaggeration, and the name is satisfactory as long as we do not understand it to imply anything far-fetched. Extend the speaker's line of thought beyond the point to which he has taken it and the result is often illuminating. It also advances the conversation and may introduce a welcome witticism to lighten it.

What is meant may be illustrated by the conversation

between Charles II and John Milton, in which the king attempted to rebuke the poet because he had written in support of Charles I's execution. The king suggested to Milton that his blindness might well be a divine punishment for his approval of what had been done by the regicides. Milton replied, "Sir, it is true that I have lost my eyesight. But if all calamitous providences are to be considered as divine judgments, your Majesty should remember that your father lost his head."

Notice how this reply keeps (economically) to the two main points of Chares II's attack. It introduces nothing new but merely extends the king's line of thought.

This method of repartee is excellent because it is allied to a way of thinking which is sound and reliable. Often we are able to see the fault in an argument only if we extend it to its logical conclusion. By carrying an observation to its conclusion, or at least further towards that end, we not only find the answer to it (and it may be one of agreement instead of disagreement) but also the perfect form in which to express it. We arrive at an answer which is logically sound and conversationally admirable.

The rest of this chapter may be devoted to a fuller treatment of suggestions already outlined, together with various other items which may encourage the more diffident, especially those who feel that such adornments as repartee or other form of wit is beyond their capacity.

With this purpose in mind consider the question of preparation. Those who study reported conversations may assume that the originals were carefully revised and polished before they were allowed to appear in print. This is true of many *Letters* and even of certain reported conversations appearing in autobiographies. As a rule, however, the fact is that most of the best conversations of which we have record were written down exactly as they were spoken. This may be a disconcerting fact but it is true. Discouragement may well come from it, since it is natural if we believe that there are people who can extemporaneously talk with the brilliance of Oscar Wilde, Dr. Johnson, Sidney Smith or G. K. Chesterton. In comparison with these giants we rightly feel that conversational ability is definitely wanting in us. The quickness of thought, the sharpness of perception, the perfect suitability of wit and reply, the timing of remarks to follow each other so that each shows the perfection of the other. These things, the inquirer properly concludes, are almost superhuman and certainly are not his either to command by intellectual gifts or by study and effort.

This depressing conclusion is based on a mistake or, more accurately, a confusion of thought. It is certainly true that many eminent conversationalists talked as they are reported. Yet it does not follow from this, as we assume it to, that what they said was wholly extemporaneous. They spoke immediately but not necessarily by inspiration. What they said was in many instances laboriously prepared.

IMPORTANCE OF TIMING REMARKS

You probably realise that the right timing of remarks is as important to a conversationalist as it is to a comedian or an actor. From observation you will have decided that one of the differences between a first-class comedian and his inferiors is that his sallies come at the right moments and to strike us just when the new twist of meaning will drive us into an even greater paroxysm of laughter. Perhaps you have experienced the result of bad timing in telling some joke of your own. A remark which you know was extremely funny has fallen flat; perhaps it was introduced when interest in the subject it referred to had flagged, or possibly because it was recounted before the subject had been developed far enough for its full signifi-

cance to be appreciated. This is a lesson which can be
noted in passing.

Now people who are careful with their conversation not
only prepare their remarks beforehand but choose the
right moment for introducing them. It is interesting to
read that Oscar Wilde was once accompanied, among
other mixed company on a ramble, by a lady who was
little capable of appreciating his conversational gifts. The
rest of the company enjoyed watching him shaping the
conversation and leading it towards a climax in which,
as their experience of him assured them, one of his
glittering aphorisms would be neatly fitted into place.
As that climax arrived the lady asked a question not only
foolish in itself but wholly irrelevant.

Wilde accepted the defeat meekly and the conversation
drifted away on to another topic. What he had in mind
to say will never be known. No doubt he found it useful
on another occasion but for this time Wilde was forced to
leave his *bon mot* unspoken and rather than introduce it
at any other than a perfectly suitable place, he was
content to leave in apparent waste all his work in building
up the conversation.

This is in the tradition of all good conversationalists.
Tom Moore, the poet, relates that Sheridan would wait
through the whole of an evening's conversation before
selecting the right moment to make the remark which he
had prepared as his contribution to what he expected
would be under discussion.

Similar care has been shown by men distinguished for
their powers of repartee, although not in themselves
outstandingly witty. Incredible as it may sound, repartee
is not always a sign of quick thinking. Some of its best
exponents are men who both think and speak slowly.
Their secret lies in the last two words, for these people
speak slowly in order that they may have time to think.

They need time to understand the full import of what is said to them and by dividing and perhaps re-dividing the thoughts of their companions, form their own opinion with its best expression in words.

This process does not detract from the merit of their conversation. Quickness of reply may often win applause because it attracts attention, as anything swift and glittering will do. Yet it is true that speed has little to do with repartee or any part of conversation. No one having any genuine appreciation of the art of talking would suggest that a man's remarks are less interesting or valuable because he makes them a few seconds later than he would have done were he possessed of a quicker mind.

To think and speak quickly should not be among the aims of those who wish to improve their conversation. Speed of thought and speedy selection of effective words will come naturally through practice. They need not be objectives to be secured by special effort. Too often people create for themselves difficulties which should not exist such as the illusion that they cannot become good conversationalists. They imagine they must become rapid talkers which is not so at all.

CONVERSATION IN COLD STORE

Far better than worrying about failure is to start keeping a notebook by the aid of which conversation may be prepared. As will be more apparent presently, all manner of uses can be found for such a book; for the moment we will remark only that it can be a useful repository for those specimens of "after-wit" which become the timely answers of future days. Here you can record improved versions of things you have said or might have said. You can note corrections you may find necessary to statements which you have made.

Finding your own faults is the best way of learning.

The entries will be original and will have the benefit of reconsideration as often as you look through the book. Such revision does not in any way deprive the entry of its freshness or spontaneity when it comes to be spoken. On the contrary, these qualities may be acquired because of the revision, with its pruning of a phrase, removal of an unnecessary word or substitution of a sharper, clearer word for one which is blurred in outline. Is this too much work? Not if conversation is your hobby. This notebook is the workshop where the tools of your craft carefully fashion the products of your art.

In addition to filing original comments and ideas you may note the sayings of other people. Some of these will come to you by your reading, listening to the wireless or from conversation. Notes of material which is not original provide you with matter for reflection. Without infringement of copyright or permission you cannot quote second-hand but you can compile a mass of worthwhile matter which will mature in your mind until it slowly becomes assimilated and blended in with your own thought. You will find that your mind has thus been enriched by it and even that the verbal forms of your expression have been improved by studying the methods and phrases of others.

This point recurred recently when a man remarked, "However it may be with others, I like my life to run along comfortable grooves. I feel well settled in them and can go along in my own way." His companion was of a more adventurous type, since he commented, "It has always seemed to me that the only difference between a groove and a grave is in depth."

Was this entirely original? Not really. But it was the spontaneous reaction of one character to another and it expressed itself in a form which the speaker may have acquired from his father, for all fathers have these "family" sayings, or from a periodical, or from some source which he had completely forgotten. The point about it is that it was almost certainly familiar material produced the more quickly for having been in stock as an idea if not as a phrase.

RESERVES OF THOUGHT AND CONFIDENCE

In the same way every conversationalist should have a reserve of thought and words which will come to him aptly as required. The building up of reserve is interesting and important. What has matured in the mind until it is a part of you cannot easily be lost. It will not vanish in any excitement or distraction which sometimes accompany a conversation. It forms the basis of self-confidence. You remain master of your tongue and to that extent of the conversation. It is not a question of inspired thinking or speedy intervention so much as of the assurance which results from a well-stored mind and practice in expression.

CHAPTER VII

APHORISM AND EPIGRAM

AFTER considering carefully how you may develop ability for repartee let us pass on to the allied subject of aphorism—pithy and arresting saying—often inaccurately termed epigram. In moving from one to the other, I may briefly repeat that the *inspiration* essential to wit cannot be taught. This fact might easily cause pessimism in many of us were it not equally true that few people are devoid of some aptitude for witticism and this can be strengthened.

If you doubt this, an experiment will prove it. Should you be one of the many who say, "I can never hope to take a part in bright conversation because I cannot say anything suitable myself", do not come to a decision until you have made this simple test.

Consider this definition: *Tact is the art of refusing a drink without losing it.*

If a companion said that, in the course of conversation, would you appreciate it?

There can only be one answer. This remark would have appealed to you partly because it is true and partly because it is amusingly expressed. You find the same type of qualities in the American advertisement for a new razor blade, "The greatest invention since the face," and in Ralph Waldo Emerson's statement that, "Every reform was once a private opinion."

WIT EXPLAINED AND DEVELOPED

Notice that in this pair of quotations only one is

amusing. Wit is not necessarily amusing but may perhaps be best understood through the definition that it is "the knife which sharpens truth to a point". It is a crisp and clear way of saying something, which such originality as may arrest and commend itself to the memory. That is why the aphorism is a good test of whether you have the quality of wit or not. If you have found the quotations so far given attractive, you have within you the qualities which ensure that you can develop your own ability to speak similarly. You will find that if you set about the task methodically, your latent ability to brighten your conversation by wit in its various forms will become active.

The first step to take is to make yourself familiar with what others have done in this way. Taking aphorisms as a material for study, read what is recorded of the wit of famous talkers, public speakers, and writers. Later in this chapter a short collection of sayings is given, varying in value as well as in their appeal to different types of mind. Read through it slowly, pausing whenever one of the quotations commends itself to you. Try to discover why it has made an impression on you.

Then see whether you can improve on it, not necessarily by saying exactly the same thing in a different form but perhaps by expressing neatly and arrestingly your own reaction to what you have read. If at first your pencil remains idle, do not be discouraged. The purpose of the exercise is not the improvement of what is quoted but the beginning of your own effort to speak briefly and originally. It is by practice as well as study that you improve in pithy and clear expression.

All this work must be done slowly. First you must steep yourself in the sayings of others. A book of quotations makes fascinating reading but you can get along very well without one, since to-day there are many periodicals which add quoted snippets to their pages. Some of the popular *Digests*, for example, may provide in one issue enough aphorisms for a week's study. Make the wit of others your familiar atmosphere. Once it has lost its strangeness, once you begin really to feel at home in it, you will find that your own wit will begin to stir.

You will find that you are acquiring the power to express yourself more perfectly, and as a consequence, more strikingly. You will be making the first, possibly the rather embarrassing and unsteady steps, towards your goal.

The next step is more experimental but one need not hold back from it, since with some conversationalists it has been the secret of their reputation for wit, in its more skilful and mature accomplishments. Here, of course, we deal with the most elementary and even crude form which is the beginning of the matter. It is a highly useful exercise.

ADAPTING APHORISMS

It consists in altering words of certain more or less accepted aphorisms. For example, take the definition which says that *Discretion is the gift which comes to a man when he is too old to need it.*

Do you agree? Many believe that is true. I once knew a quiet young man who did not, at least in any universal application. The saying was a favourite with an elderly man whom I personally did not find pleasant or trustworthy and, as it proved, this young man held the same opinion. No one suspected this until one day during a luncheon his elderly companion called on him for "a few words". It was a wretchedly unfair thing to do, for the youngster was no speaker and he was among men who mostly could speak extemporarily with ease and humour.

However, the challenge was accepted quietly and the young man spoke for perhaps two minutes—on "Discretion". No one had the least doubt whom the remarks were addressed to. "I am trying to remember," he said presently, "a quotation about discretion which has always seemed to me particularly striking. Although I have heard X quote it many a time, I cannot. . . . Ah, yes, it is that discretion is a gift which . . . comes to a man . . . when he is too old . . . to *use* it."

If ever a man had his nose twisted in public, his elderly acquaintance experienced humiliation that day. Some years later I came across the unwilling young speaker again. Then he was addressing delighted audiences all the year round, and earning large fees by doing so.

Here we have an example of a man who, familiar with one saying and many times turning it over distrustfully in his mind, had suddenly seen that by altering one word he could express a totally different meaning. Had he ever contemplated using it? Probably not, but when the oppotunity was forced upon him, he not only used it with effect but to the final release of the powers which he, less than anyone, suspected to be in him.

There is the danger that to handle anything epigrammatic in this way is like playing games which will reduce the art of concise and crisp expression into mere mechanical routine. Yet an awareness of the danger is enough to keep one perpetually on guard against it and to prevent one from contracting a habit in which all ingenuity of form is without any life or inspired thought.

This is proved by the fact that many conversationalists have used this method without destroying their powers. It was often the method behind Oscar Wilde's best remembered aphorisms, e.g., "An honest God's the noblest work of man." One may not see the point of the saying in its context, or one may not agree with what it states, but we must admit that it perfectly expresses the cynical point of view.

The insincere or artificial must be avoided, because it is wrong in itself and also because it can only do harm to conversation. It can be said that those who have indulged in the merely startling have not *by that means* enhanced their reputation as conversationalists, although they may have enjoyed a temporary popularity as entertainers. We may still laugh at or savour the quip, but we may not allow ourselves to confuse isolated and entertaining epigram with the right use of aphorisms in conversation. Now turn to the examples which are set out below. After considering a method by which you may increase your ability, it will be wise to begin to practise the lesson. As a preliminary to this, these examples will get you into the right mood for the work.

The quotations have been grouped under general headings, although some of them could have been classified under more than one of the groups.

PROGRESS. SUCCESS.
"When I came to this country, I hadn't a nickel in my pocket. Now I have a nickel in my pocket."
Groucho Marx.

"Only those who have stopped thinking, or who never started, boast of never having changed their minds."
Dwight MacDonald.

"Progress is impossible without change, and those who cannot change their minds cannot change anything."
George Bernard Shaw.

"The man who never alters his opinion is like standing water, and breeds only reptiles of the mind."
William Blake.

"The three most important bones are the wishbone, the jawbone, and the backbone. The first spurs you on, the second helps you find out, and the third keeps you at it."   *New Zealand Weekly News.*

"Assurance is two-thirds of success."   *Gaelic Proverb.*

"But, Lord! to see what success do, whether with or without reason, and making a man seem wise."   *Pepys' Diary*, Aug. 15, 1666.

"The only infallible criterion of wisdom to vulgar judgments—success."   *Edmund Burke.*

"Progress stops when it ceases to possess individuality."   *John Stuart Mill.*

WOMEN
"He who heeds the advice of a woman is a fool; he who heeds it not is lost."   *Spanish Proverb.*

"Great-grandmama was adorable; Grandmama was quaint; Mother is old-fashioned."   *Anonymous.*

"A little girl said, ' I know something I won't talk about.' Her father said, 'When you grow up, it will be the other way about'."

"Friends—two women angry with the same person."   *English Digest.*

"I don't know how you put up with that idle husband of yours."
"It's like this, mum. I make our living and he makes life worth living."

"Women read men more truly than men read women."   *Charlotte Brontë.*

"Women are born worshippers."   *Thomas Carlyle.*

FRIENDSHIP.
"When you are down and out, something always turns up—and it's usually the noses of your friends."   *Orson Welles.*

"It is better to grow a branch than cut off a limb."   *Chinese Proverb.*

"It is always better to discuss what is right rather than who is right."   *Anonymous.*

"A man, sir, should keep his friendship in constant repair."   *Samuel Johnson.*

ADVERTISEMENT
"Promise, large promise, is the soul of an advertisement."   *Samuel Johnson.*

BUSINESS, etc.
"Business? It is a simple matter; it is other people's money."   *Dumas the Younger.*

"October is one of the peculiarly dangerous months to speculate in stocks in. The next most dangerous months are the other eleven."   *Based on Mark Twain.*

"The wise man makes hay of the grass that grows under the other man's feet."   *English Digest.*

"When a man is no longer anxious to do better than well, he is done for."   *Benjamin Haydon.*

F

COMPLACENCY

"Let us not be too particular. It is better to have old second-hand diamonds than none at all."

Mark Twain.

"A great many persons are able to become members of this House without losing their insignificance."

Beverley Baxter, M.P.

"To love oneself is the beginning of a life-long romance."   *Oscar Wilde.*

"There isn't a parallel of latitude but thinks it would have been the equator if it had its rights." *Mark Twain.*

MARRIAGE

"There swims no goose so grey but soon or late,
She finds some honest gander for her mate."

Geoffrey Chaucer.

"A married man acquires a large vocabulary—by marrying it."   *Louie Ronson.*

"A good marriage would be between a blind wife and a deaf husband."   *Montaigne (Essais, Book 3, ch. VI).*

"A married man is a bachelor whose luck has failed him."   *Anonymous.*

"Love is like war; you begin when you like and leave off when you can."   *Swanson Newsette.*

MAN.

"Man is a creature who lives not upon bread alone, but principally by catchwords." *Robert Louis Stevenson.*

"He sows hurry and reaps indigestion."
Robert Louis Stevenson.

"All the world is a little mad except you and I. And even you are a little mad."   *Old Saying.*

VIEWPOINTS

"To know what we know, and know what we do not know, that is wisdom."   *Confucius.*

"It is never unlucky to turn back if you are on the wrong road."   *Anonymous.*

"Don't worry if you go bald. Just imagine if they ached and you had to have them out like teeth."
Anonymous.

"What cannot be repaired is not to be regretted."
Samuel Johnson.

"A gentleman considers what is right; the small man considers what will pay."   *Confucius.*

"Humble because of knowledge; mighty by sacrifice."
Rudyard Kipling.

"A classic is something by a dead Englishman or a live foreigner."   *Anonymous.*

ASPECTS OF LIFE

"There are two things to aim at in life; first, to get what you want; and after that to enjoy it. Only the wisest of mankind achieve the second."
Logan Pearsall Smith.

"I rather pride myself on knowing when to stand on my dignity and when to sit on it."

John Galsworthy (*A Family Man, Act I*).

"I never saw such sad faces and such gay behinds."

Marshal Foch (after a visit to a Variety theatre).

"There is only one rule about income. Make it first and make it last."

Anonymous.

In reading through these examples you will have found that some of them remain easily in the memory. Perhaps these are sayings which you will wish to use in conversation and with proper acknowledgment where this may be due.

If this is so, why not increase the number of sayings for yourself? Make your own compilation of aphorisms, noting down those which appeal to you personally or which seem to illustrate your views or to destroy the opinions you disagree with. Each time you hear or read a saying which appeals to you, jot it down. In the words of Captain Cuttle, "When found, make a note of." The more varied your list, the more useful it will be to you, ranging from "A boy is an appetite inside a skin" to "History repeats itself, but it puts the price up every time."

In using your aphorisms be careful not to drag them in as often as you can. Brief sayings should be used sparingly if they are to retain their effectiveness, and especially those which are thoughtful.

In conversation a judicious use of aphorism makes unnecessary that long and laboured talking by which a point may be established or a meaning defined. Any good conversationalist will have available from his repertoire a story or a saying which will briefly and clearly cut through the tangle of words and put his idea forward unmistakably and pleasantly. This means both that those who like to hear themselves talk can be kept in check and that the speaker's own view is sure of attention. Charles Lamb wrote that some people disliked talking to Elia because of his ability to take their long speeches out of their mouths and express their meaning briefly. In spite of his impediment of speech, Lamb was a brilliant talker although he rarely spoke at length, and it is interesting to find this comment by Hazlitt on one feature of his conversation:—"He would interrupt the gravest conversation with some light jest; and yet, perhaps, not quite irrelevant in the ears that could understand it. Your long and much talkers hated him."

Here we perceive a twofold advantage in the use of aphorism. One is that you may prevent anyone from deadening the conversation by excessive talking, by intervening yourself as often as may be necessary yet without occupying too much time. The other advantage is that, at least in the earlier stages of your progress, the use of the brief sayings of others will not only help to teach you correctness of timing but will enable you to develop your own habit of brief utterance.

Finally some readers will be interested to note that the use of aphorism gives them the advantage of being the better able to start a conversation.

EASY START TO A CONVERSATION

We have already considered in great detail a method by which the difficulty of opening a conversation with one who is more or less a stranger may be overcome. Now we may add the advice that is often wise to make your conversational approach by means of a short and striking saying. If you have read Bacon's *Essays* you may have noticed how often he sustains interest or opens it out by the introduction of a pithy maxim.

For the conversationalist this is even more useful than it is to the essayist, for it is impossible to compress your meaning into a short phrase unless you have thought it out. The use of aphorism guarantees thinking, and therefore conveys immediately to the person you address that your remark is not lightly made. If you have one or two remarks of topical interest, and possibly of different application, ready for the opening of a conversation you will find that your partner will respond to one of them, if not to the first. What you say is necessarily interesting and stimulating, because it is in the form of an aphorism. Consequently its qualities bring a reaction; the man you speak to will be impelled to reply, so that your opening now has the chance to grow into a conversation.

In this connexion there is a certain amount of Hazlitt's quiet humour in his advice, "If you really want to know whether another person can talk well, begin by saying a good thing yourself, and you will have the right to look for a rejoinder."

At the opening of this chapter it was stated that an aphorism is sometimes wrongly called epigram. This usage is now so frequent that it would be pedantic to insist on the distinction, at least in everyday speech. Nevertheless, it is to our purpose to look at the epigram properly so called in the original sense of the word. This meant "a short poem", especially one containing a statement refined to conciseness. Conington's well-known translation of the epitaph ascribed to Simonides of Chios (d. 469 B.C.) is a good example:—

"Go tell the Spartans, thou that passest by,
That here, obedient to their laws, we lie."

It is evident that any saying so brief and metrical, and from which every unnecessary word has been excluded, is both easy to remember and incisive in use. The epigram is therefore an ideal means for expressing yourself clearly, pleasantly, and effectively. The same is true of most short jingles and we often use them in social life, as one who refuses cheese after lunch and murmurs,

> "Now cheese it is a peevish elf,
> Digesting all things but itself."

In conversation such verses are most useful and the epigram is the most useful of all, for its force comes at the end. Therefore there is something decisive in its employment. This was noted by Lillius Gyraldus in the tenth *Dialogue* of his *De Poetarum Historia* (1545), where he observes, "Others liken the epigram to a Scorpion, which, although every part of it is to be dreaded, yet has the poison in his tail, wherein is the sting."

For material of this kind obviously one must go to the famous epigrammatists or be alert to note down such epigrams as one may hear or come across in general reading. The wise student will make good use of the poems of Alexander Pope, which abound in epigrams such as,

> "In Faith and Hope the world will disagree,
> But all mankind's concern is Charity."

> "On life's vast ocean diversely we sail,
> Reason the card, but passion is the gale."

> "Avoid extremes; and shun the fault of such
> Who still are pleased too little or too much."

> "Such laboured nothings, in so strange a style,
> Amaze the unlearn'd, and make the learned smile."

"Some praise at morning what they blame at night,
But always think the last opinion right."

It would be possible to fill a small book with such epigrams from Pope, but we must leave him after a final quotation which has special value for conversationalists—

"Men must be taught as if you taught them not,
And things unknown proposed as things forgot."

The epigram is not necessarily as short as those printed above, as we see by a quotation from Winthrop Mackworth Praed's *The Vicar*,

"His talk was like a stream which runs
With rapid change from rocks to roses;
It slipped from politics to puns:
It passed from Mahomet to Moses."

From the same author we may also select,

"And when religious sects ran mad,
He held, in spite of all their learning,
That if man's belief is bad,
It will not be improved by burning."

A few more quotations may be found useful to start you off on your own collection.

"God bless the king, I mean the faith's defender;
God bless—no harm in blessing—the pretender;
Who that pretender is, and who is king,
God bless us all, that's quite another thing."

John Byron.

"Swift flies each tale of laughter, shame, or folly,
Caught by Paul Pry, and carried home to Dolly."

Charles Sprague.

"Oh, spare your idol! Think him human still;
Charms he may have, but he has frailties too;
Dote not too much, nor spoil what ye admire."

William Cowper.

"Though man a thinking being is defined,
Few use the great prerogative of mind.
How few think justly of the thinking few!
How many never think, who think they do!"

Jane Taylor.

"Treason doth never prosper: what's the reason?
For if it prosper, none dare call it treason."

Sir John Harrington.

"He slept beneath the moon,
He basked beneath the sun;
He lived a life of going-to-do,
And died with nothing done."   *James Albery.*

"Time to me this truth has taught
('Tis a treasure worth revealing),
More offend from want of thought,
Than from any want of feeling."

Charles Swain.

Enough has now been written and illustrated to make you feel at home in practising the use of aphorism and epigram. Alertness of thought, crispness and originality of expression, and freshness in use, are the main requisites, as we may set out in Yeats's lines.

> "A line may take us hours maybe,
>   Yet, if it does not seem a moment's thought,
>   Our stitching and unstitching has been naught."

CHAPTER VIII

THE USE OF ANECDOTE

MOST good conversationalists are also good *raconteurs*; they can almost always tell a story which is new, interesting, and importantly, illuminating.

Whatever the topic of conversation, they can illustrate what they wish to say by putting it in story form. This is certainly of great value to them, for not only does everyone love a story but everyone remembers a story—and its point—better than a bare statement. This is why Robert Louis Stevenson, in praising the ambition to be a good conversationalist, accorded equal praise to the talker's desire to "have a fact, a thought, an illustration pat to every subject".

The ability to excel in this way depends on two things: the possession of a fund of good stories and the knowledge of how anecdotes should be told.

The first is easily obtained. Every week both the radio and the printed periodicals pour out hundreds of first-class stories most suitable for the conversationalist. Compilations of stories useful to public speakers are valuable to the conversationalist, although here, where you buy in bulk, it may be as well to warn the inexperienced that cheaper publications of broad grins yield little good material. You are not looking for the belly-laugh or sex type of story, but only for anecdotes, such as those taken from the sayings or actions of real people, which are capable of illustrating a point. What the girl said when the bathroom curtain fell down is best forgotten; if you have in hand something said by Beatrice Lillie, Monty Woolley, Marc Connelly, Dorothy Parker, Alexander Woollcott, Rebecca West, Fanny Brice, or if you know Elsa Maxwell's three word secret for making a guest feel at home, you have something which will be useful for the rest of your life.

Of course, there are many people who can reel off story after story, keeping us all thoroughly amused or otherwise entertained for a couple of hours. But "useful yarns" are not exactly what you are looking for. What you require is a notebook *memorandum* of stories which either illustrate some point or are capable of being used as illustrations. That is to say, there must be in the anecdote a "moral" which is arresting, apart from the humour or pathos, of the story in itself. Each of the following anecdotes stands by itself or may be used to exemplify a variety of ideas. They are typical of stories which have circulated in recent years.

Anxious to settle reports that he was unsympathetic towards religion, Herr Goering announced that he would present a statue to a church already under construction. A competition was opened for designs, which Herr Goering would himself judge to ensure that the statue was in every way suitable. For six months designs poured in, representing the Founder of Christianity, German saints, St. Peter, the martyrdom of St. Stephen, St. John at the foot of the Cross, Mary Magdalene breaking the vase of spikenard, and a variety of Biblical scenes and miracles. Every week Herr Goering sat down to look through the latest arrivals, and ruled most of them out on the spot. As the competition drew to its close his staff began to feel considerable alarm. Then came the happy day when a beam of intense satisfaction appeared on the

Marshal's face and spread happily as he gazed at a large sheet of paper. Peering over his massive shoulders, his assistants saw that here was a full-length drawing of the Marshal himself, in full uniform and covered with medals, reading a very small book marked, "New Testament".

When England became one-hundred-per-cent Socialist and devotion to factory production was the only virtue remaining, a man went to work one morning and was alarmed to find that his three mates had all been shot the previous evening. "Why?" he asked, astonished. "What had they done?" The foreman explained. "Smith was always fifteen minutes late. They shot him for sabotaging the production effort. Jones was always punctual. They shot him for plotting against the State—no man can be dead punctual all the time unless he's up to something. Brown was always fifteen minutes early, so he was shot for political unreliability. You can't trust a man who is toadying up to the management."

Some time ago a young man was committed by his family to a mental home. This greatly upset a wealthy friend of his, who immediately started spending a good deal of time and money to secure his release. After nearly two years of patient effort he succeeded in lining up three psychiatrists who testified that the young fellow was completely normal and always had been. The friend carried the doctors and the ex-patient off to his flat for dinner and celebration. Before the evening was over he asked, "What are you going to do now? Go away for a holiday, I suppose, and then settle down as before." "Well, I thought of getting something to do, actually," was the reply. "Something quiet, of course, but interesting. Like writing a book.

I have not really made up my mind whether to do that or take up painting again. On the other hand, of course, I might just go on being a tea-cosy."

Stories about psychiatrists are innumerable, of course, and most of them remain current because there are so many quack "psychologists" in practice, and because comparatively few people know what a psychiatrist actually does. He probably does not know himself. These stories will lose value if the science becomes more widely understood. In the meantime, the very best of them are in reasonably good taste but the others surely weaken rather than help any use to which they may be put. Perhaps one my be allowed to reprint one which has more than one point. It is contained in two letters.

"Dear Joe,
We have been very worried lately about my brother. He came in one night and said someone had waited for him outside the office. We were upset. Each evening he said the same thing, so we persuaded him to consult a psychiatrist, who said it wasn't very serious yet and was due to overwork. The treatment didn't do any good, because my brother began to think the man was following him through the streets. All the family have been terribly worried and really dreaded my brother's coming home, especially after he said the man had followed him right to the front door. We do hope things won't get any worse . . . if they can. What do you think?"

"Dear Joe,
Mike won't be writing to you this month. He followed me home from work last night and managed to catch the fellow who's been following me around lately. The

THE USE OF ANECDOTE

police say he's got three convictions already for knocking people on the head. So Mike won't be writing you for a while. He and the rest of the family have gone off to consult a different psychiatrist."

If that one doesn't appeal to you, you may find a use for the one about the man who bored his acquaintances badly one evening by his quiet but persistent stories about himself. All these summed up to the line that he was quite a wonder-boy; there wasn't anything he couldn't do or hadn't done when called upon. No one quite knew how to dam his slow flood of egotism. Then somebody said . . .

"The grimmest fix I was ever in was the time I was wrecked on a tiny island. It was last year. I was on a friend's yacht when it sank without warning . . . boiler blew up or something . . . and there I was on this little island, with not another living thing surviving but my friend's two parrots. I was there eight days before I was rescued. By that time, I'd had to eat both parrots."

No one knew how to handle this situation either, since it was broken off just when it was poised for action. The speaker looked steadily at the wondering bore.

"That's how I became the only man in the world with the habit of sampling parrot flesh," he went on sombrely. "On my island I longed for duck and green peas, turkey and bread sauce, chicken with crisps of bacon. . . . And those two parrots could *imitate* anything."

Well, there are many ways of scoring in conversation

and of changing the subject. Evidently that is one of them. And from these examples you see what is meant by the rule that an anecdote must have point in itself as well as a significance relating to the topic under discussion. A story should never be told wholly for its own sake, however good it may be in itself, since alone it is merely entertaining. *If a story is told in conversation, it should link up with what is being said.*

Its point must be quickly seen—as a rule, although there is the delayed action story which is most effective and requires expert telling—and should not require comment by way of explanation. If explanatory remark is needed it should come before the story. This must be done, for example, if the point of the story depends on characterization; in this case, you should briefly make listeners familiar with the characters you are going to use.

WAIT TILL THE RIGHT TIME

Do not be in a hurry to tell your story as soon as it comes into your mind. Wait to choose the right moment. If the conversation takes an unforeseen rush beyond that point or veers abruptly off to another topic, do not interrupt to get the story in. To do this is to lose most of the effectiveness, because you are now drawing people's attention to something they have already considered, possibly inadequately, but that is irrelevant. The freshness has gone off the topic and you should be content to leave it alone. Keep your story for another day, which may come sooner than expected. Conversation often eddies round like a tide and comes back naturally to where it was earlier. If it does not do this, let the story go and reflect to see where your timing went wrong.

This matter of timing has already been dealt with when we were thinking about aphorisms, but we may repeat here that it is vitally important in the telling of anecdotes. Here one has to consider not only the right instant for introducing the story but also the timing of the narration. Entertainers know that any story will fail if its internal timing is faulty. If you want to learn the lesson well, pay attention to the telling of humorous stories on the radio. Some jokes turn up fairly often, started by the experts and drifting thereafter through many degrees to the amateurs of works' canteens. You will notice how the jokes and quips of the top-liners are harassed, pale, over-worked, and creaky when produced by "Mr. Blank, the cheery member of the Accounts Department". Mr. Blank will almost certainly have seen the point of the story but his efforts to rediscover it are so prolonged and jerky that the story becomes painfully tedious. That is why we have so much of this sort of thing.

"Talking of mermaids, I went down to Brighton the other day. Oh, yes, I went to Brighton . . . lovely place . . . very jolly. . . . Well, when I got to Brighton. . . ."

Even some of our most highly-paid "comics" work up their stories and audiences by pitiful efforts like this. Using these as the "awful warnings", we should study the methods of the "shining examples" who add each detail at exactly the right moment to cause the greatest desired effect at that instant, the whole building up to complete success, for the climax. Do not delay a story till it grows chilly, or hurry through it almost unnoticed.

EXPERIMENT ON FRIENDS

Professional and amateur *raconteurs* find that the right timing of a story is acquired only by practical experience. There is nothing discouraging in this. It means that you should tell a story which appeals to you when told by

G

an expert and then notice that your narrative isn't as good as his. Try such a story on your friends. What goes wrong with it? Are you using too many words? Have you altered the exact position of the climax? Are you making too much of the details, perhaps making them so effective that the climax doesn't stand out sufficiently? Is your pace throughout too irregular, too slow, too rapid? By such questions you will surely master the timing which is so necessary.

You will probably be helped by observing a few *do's* and *don'ts*.

SOME DON'TS

For instance, your story should be brief. It is true that some stories are very lengthy. The celebrated story about "the wood-shove" would require several pages of this book. And these stories may be useful in conversation; as a rule, however, their value is in entertainment only. Usually, keep your anecdote as short as possible because brevity has an effectiveness of its own which will go a long way towards making the story successful.

Another point to watch is the correct placing of the climax. Work in every detail necessary to it beforehand. That sounds obvious. Notice how many times the rule is broken. At the same time, don't try to build it up too much, keeping it waiting until suspense begins to dwindle.

Your story should never depend for effect on anything which may be unfamiliar to your audience. One of the best stories I know is pointless unless you know the use of fracture boards. It is an excellent story to tell among doctors or nurses or people trained in first aid; in other company it requires a preliminary explanation, so that the immediacy of the effect is destroyed at the beginning.

Another way in which unfamiliarity may spoil effectiveness is found in those stories which depend on the oddity or originality or other personal quality of someone un-known to your listeners. We have often had to listen to a story about someone and thought it definitely second-rate, an impression which was in no way diminished when the narrator said, "But you should have seen him yourself . . . if you had *heard* him saying it . . . you'd have found it too funny for words." This "he ought to be on the stage" kind of story should be avoided, unless you have marked gifts as an impersonator.

We have two more *don'ts* to deal with. You should not use too much detail. If a story demands an elaborate setting, the painting of a detailed picture or the establishment of considerable background, it is more suited to writing than to speaking. Remember, as a general rule, that a spoken story does not hold audience-interest for more than about two hundred words. Of course an experienced *raconteur* can dispense with this rule. Simplicity of situation and dialogue are therefore essential to any story.

Our second caution is best expressed positively. We may do this by saying that if, in the telling of a story, you find that some explanatory detail is needed, where you did not expect to be called on to supply it, try to slip in the information as if it were accidental. Put in a hesitation, for example, as if you had momentarily forgotten an item or couldn't recall a name. This is a very useful trick if you notice that your audience is not *au fait* with what you are talking about. It will occasionally happen that someone you are talking with will not have the general knowledge which you happen to have and your story may then well need a little extra help. This can be illustrated by an anecdote which has been printed and often recounted. I last heard it told to a number of school-children. Notice how the narrator made sure that even the slowest of them would appreciate the point when it came, by pretending a hesitation at the beginning, under cover of which he gave the climax the background it needed. By the way, the youngsters had been talking about the way in which famous people slip out of the news and become "nobodies" almost in a night.

MORE ADVANCED METHODS

Now let us turn away from cautionary rules. By observation of the work of others and by your own self-criticism, you will be able to pass from short and straightly told anecdotes to those needing more skill, and you will certainly find that you have now the ability to indulge in some of the tricks of the trade. A quick opening may be followed by a leisurely sentence or two, seemingly almost irrelevant but actually calculated to heighten the climax to follow. These slower periods enable the listeners to collect their wits, to pick up and appreciate the point given in the opening, and to see for themselves, without your having to waste words on it, a point which they will themselves link up with the climax, to its greater effect.

Your instinct for appreciating and telling a good story will increase and you will gain confidence as you find your judgment more reliable.

Part of this development will come by rehearsal. In the course of this chapter you have doubtless realized that only rarely can a beginner leave the telling of a story to the inspiration of the moment. A story needs rehearsal. Probably only a few people will be surprised to know that many of the best story-tellers go over their best items repeatedly. The pause which comes pat at the right place, the tiny explanatory phrase slipped in unnoticeably, the hint of a smile which heightens suspense and indicates, "It's coming now . . ." the sudden mimicry which makes a character come to life, all these and other aids occur so naturally that we may overlook the fact that they have been acquired by patient work. Now the *raconteur* may be such a master that he can do what he likes, telling every story with the knowledge that he will add every touch which it needs, in any company, but he was not always so expert. His eminence is due to the patient labour with which he laid its foundations.

You need not feel inferior because you have to learn. Your target is to make your stories spontaneous in the telling, whether they are humorous or not. The means by which we accomplish this aim are deliberate and practised, nor should anyone think otherwise unless he believes that a concert pianist never sits at the keyboard except on the platform, or that a conjuror's tricks are not prepared for months, maybe years.

When you talk you should be two people. One the person by whose knowledge and skill a real contribution is made to the conversation, the man who supplies the facts, the illustrations, the words. The other should be the critic, who is always reasonably alert, noting how the other man is faring and giving him a hint now and again, observing why he succeeds here or why he fails there. This is the man who has the ultimate enjoyment, for in every art there are two pleasures. One is the enjoyment of doing, of making, of using acquired skill. The other is the joy of noticing how this skill is succeeding in reaching its objective, or in analysing where, why and how it failed to do so. This isn't serious, unless we take ourselves too seriously about life itself. It is rather the all-embracing joy of genius, and I think it is summed up in the comment of a waiter at a London hotel, who is on record as saying of G. K. Chesterton, "Your friend he a very clever man. He sit and laugh. And then he write. And then he laugh at what he write."

Need one add anything to that picture of a man who knew how to write because he had learnt how to write and now enjoyed doing what was to him a labour which was of his very nature?

With experience will come the ability to develop stories of your own. How you handled this or that situation; what you said when the lawn-mower broke down or how you repaired it—subjects are endless if you but remember them—and these original stories are usually the most entertaining, if they are carefully selected and stored away for recall.

Let us sum up this chapter by quoting from Cowper's poem on *Conversation:*—

"A tale should be judicious, clear, succinct,
  The language plain, the incidents well linked;
  Tell not as new what everybody knows,
  And, new or old, still hasten to a close."

CHAPTER IX

MISCELLANEOUS METHODS AND ETIQUETTE

INTO this chapter are gathered a number of points essential to good conversation. Because they are brief, it does not follow that they are unimportant.

Not merely for the sake of repetition but to throw new light on it, we repeat the rule that every conversational topic must be well prepared. Even if it is so new that it was chosen from this morning's newspaper, or even if it is thrust upon you unexpectedly, it should be prepared in that you bring to it a well-stocked and orderly mind. Talk which is not thoughtful is frothy. It has appearance, a vague shape, but no substance. This applies to the lightest and most trivial of conversations. In other words, do not say anything until you have something to say. "Think twice before you speak once."

The necessity of thinking about a topic imposes on us the duty of having facts at our disposal. Obviously the first thing to do in approaching conversation is to call to mind all the facts we can about its topics. Whether we are expected to talk about cabbages or kings, we must know of what we talk. We cannot know this unless we have facts in mind and with them suitable details, stories, examples, and, perhaps, quotations from authorities. Notice how the people who keep a conversation going are those who continually feed the topic with new facts and ideas.

This does not mean that each of us must be a walking

encyclopedia of knowledge. It does mean that we must be reasonably well-informed persons at least in those subjects we venture to talk about. In these days of plenty, for they are truly days of plenty for anyone who wants to be factual in his statements, you can have a library of knowledge by spending two shillings a week on carefully chosen periodicals. From these gather the facts connected with the topics in which you are interested. Make notes about them, for the sake of accuracy, and file away clippings. They are your raw material.

Lord Chesterfield, whose *Letters* contain several valuable lessons and observations about the art of conversation, says that the French, "however classically ignorant they may be, think it a shame to be ignorant of the history of their own country." He continues, "They read that, if they read nothing else and having often read nothing else, are proud of having read that, and talk of it willingly; even the women are well instructed in that sort of reading."

From this the author proceeds to a warning so well expressed that it must be given *in extenso* in his own words. It puts us on our guard against talking too much and this is a necessary caution for, when we know that we have many facts with which to support our conversation, we are in danger of speaking at too great length—of overwhelming our companions with our knowledge!

"I am far from meaning by this," Lord Chesterfield continues, "that one should always be talking wisely, in company of books, history and matters of knowledge. There are many companies which you will, and ought to keep, where such conversation would be misplaced and ill-timed; your own good sense must distinguish the company and the time. You must trifle only with triflers; and be serious only with the serious, but dance to those who pipe. From the moment that you are dressed to go out, pocket all your knowledge with your watch, and never pull it out unless desired: the producing of the one unasked implies that you are weary of the company; and the producing of the other unrequired will make the company weary of you. Company is a republic too jealous of its liberties to suffer a dictator even for a quarter of an hour; and yet in that, as in all republics, there are some few who really govern; but then it is by seeming to disclaim, instead of attempting to usurp, the power: that is the occasion in which manners, address and the undefinable *je ne sais quois* triumph; if properly exerted, their conquest is sure, and the more lasting for not being perceived."

Through understanding the wisdom of this advice, famous conversationalists knew that they controlled talk as much by their silence as by their thoughtful and timely remarks. The witty Sidney Smith, for instance, never spoke for more than half a minute at a time. As he said, this gave other people a chance to talk and conversation became widespread.

AVOID BEING ASSERTIVE

Chesterfield's idea is one that should use the materials of conversation as one uses coins, in exchange for goods, buying here and there according to our judgments of the best markets. Before following him here, we may again protest against those talkers who imagine they are conversationalists because they do most of the talking. In their case, if the situation is at its worst, there may be a fulfilment of Frank Hubbard's comment that,

"Nobuddy kin talk so interestin' as th' feller that's not hampered by facts or information."

More usually, however, we find what Cowper remarked and in later lines defined:—

"Where men of judgment creep and feel their way,
The positive pronounce without dismay."

"Asseveration blustering in your face
Makes contradiction such a hopeless case."

And there we have it. People who talk emotionally but thoughtlessly often offend in this way, speaking at first from reason but on the least divergence of view, speaking with passion and heat, until all conversation dies either in a quarrel or in the desert of an endless monologue.

Remote from this is Chesterfield's idea of conversation, during which silences are used to foresee the effects of what is being said, to compare what is being expressed with what one thinks and in choosing the right time to put your own viewpoint reasonably, entertainingly if possible, and well.

During silence one should also be thinking of facts which will support the varying ideas of our companions. The purpose of this consideration is not to use them on one side or another. This would be insincere in itself and in the conversation fatally artificial. The aim in discovering and reflecting on such facts is to find out what may stimulate the thought of others. Ask the various speakers if this fact affects their opinion or is this other fact part of their conclusions. Leave these ideas to your companions to talk about, giving your own view whenever you wish. This is the way in which to handle the small change of conversation.

In making your contribution, give preference to those ideas which, as far as your knowledge of the group allows you to judge, will be of general interest. You know the interests of the people who are talking together; you know their habits of thought; you know their temperaments and natural inclinations. Make use of this knowledge as a guide in the handling of your ideas and reflections. Even if your knowledge of these things is incomplete, you should weigh them up as far as you may before deciding on what you will say yourself. This remark will probably arouse difference of opinion between A, B, and C. Do you want that? Now or later? Would it be better at this moment to stimulate a further exchange of ideas between these three before introducing the suggestion which may cause divergence? What can you do to widen the range of the conversation?

These are a few of the questions which enter you mind as you attend to what is being said, considering both what you are going to say and its possible effects. What you offer must not only be a purposeful contribution to what is said; it should also draw others into conversation between themselves.

For this purpose questions are eminently useful. They are stimulating, and, if carefully framed, lead to greater exactness of speech. Ask a speaker to define his meaning, to say exactly what he has in mind in using certain terms or phrases. Ask him how he may reconcile one fact with another. Ask for the production of facts in support of a statement.

In doing this, but be careful not to offend, for one notices some people whose conversational technique consists mostly of asking questions. This practice is bad, since it becomes apparent and then annoys. Moreover, it paralyses your own conversation. Yet once you know of it, it is useful on occasion and, at all times, it is amusing to notice how many men and women who are really of small attainment pass for highly successful conversationalists merely because they know the method. Needless to say inquisitive or impertinent questions are normally a sign of bad breeding.

If questions are used unobtrusively and not too often their function as a conversational aid may be recommended. They have an occasional but not a regular value.

They help to maintain what Lord Chesterfield terms the "fermentation" of good talk, which we are ourselves dealing with at the moment, and may help to prevent a conversation from lapsing into trivialities. With his preference for French society, he observes that, "It must be owned that the polite conversation of the men and women of fashion at Paris, although not always very deep, is much less futile and frivolous than ours here. It turns at least upon some subject, something of taste, some point of history, criticism, and even philosophy; which, though probably not quite so solid as Mr. Locke's, is however better and more becoming rational beings than our frivolous dissertations upon the weather, or upon whist."

After quoting the satirist, Charles Pineau Duclos, to the effect that there was at the time a universal and increasing ferment of reason in France, he adds, "Whereas, I am sorry to say, that here that fermentation seems to have been over some years ago, the spirit evaporated, and only the dregs left."

These are severe words and might wrongly give the impression that the noble lord was unable to enjoy the pleasures of light conversation. Yet they are true always of every manner of conversation.

DON'T BE TOO WISE

Chesterfield has something to say about the less serious exchange of ideas and as usual he is helpful. His attitude here has been foreshadowed in his words already quoted, warning us against perpetual sobriety of talking. He would not have us to be always talking too wisely nor too well.

For this master of polite usage knew that it is often necessary or desirable that we should talk about the small events of life instead of about its profound problems. He does not wish us to confine ourselves to the lessons of history or the enigmas of human nature.

He recognizes the advisability of occasionally talking "nothings", and writes, "For in some companies it would be imprudent to talk of anything else; and with many people it is impossible to talk of anything else; they would not understand you."

In a letter written fifteen months after this quotation, he returned to the point and opened it out. After referring to Descartes and Sir Isaac Newton, he declared:—

"I honour and respect such superior geniuses; but I desire to converse with people of this world, who bring into company their share, at least, of cheerfulness, good breeding, and knowledge of mankind. In common life, one much oftener wants small money, and silver, than gold. Give me a man who has ready cash about him for present expenses; sixpences, shillings, half-crowns and crowns, which circulate easily: but a man who has only an ingot of gold about him is much above common purposes, and his riches are not handy nor convenient. Have as much gold as you please in one pocket, but take care always to keep change in the other; for you will oftener have occasion for a shilling than for a guinea."

It is clear from this and earlier quotations that what has been written here, about the importance of having conversational topics already prepared, does not preclude the use of comparatively small topics on suitable occasions. For instance, when members of a group are meeting for the first time, we should be able to secure their interest and promote an exchange of ideas by proposing several subjects, which will be acceptable to all and at the same time less banal than "the weather" or recent sporting events.

LIST OF TOPICS

The conversationalist can prepare a stock of some half a dozen topics which provide pleasant and easy ways into general talking. Of this Chesterfield writes, with reference to the interesting custom of his day, "There is a fashionable kind of small talk, which you should get; which, trifling as it is, is of use in mixed companies, and at table . . . where it keeps off certain serious subjects, that might create disputes or at least coldness for a time. Upon such occasions it is not amiss to know how to *parler cuisine*, or to be able to dissert upon the growth and flavour of wines. These, it is true, are very little things; but they are little things that occur very often. . . ."

Such is the advice of a man of the world, who gave us the shrewd saying that, "Where one would gain people, remember that nothing is little."

For one whose aim is to discover the interests of others and then persuade them to talk this maxim should be unforgettable. No interest is too trivial to be unworthy of consideration.

In this connexion one may offer a suggestion which will be found useful. This is that one should have in readiness a few subjects which are slightly unusual or are in some way original. People whom we meet casually will find them refreshingly interesting and will therefore the more readily enter into talk about them. This does not suppose that we must be people of wide learning or of exceptional general knowledge, but only that we should always be alert to notice and remember these small, out-of-the-way things which catch human interest. It is almost impossible to exemplify in a short space all that is meant by this advice but here is a hint as to what may be done, taken from an actual conversation which took place in the middle of a wide and apparently empty plain crossed by an enormous railway viaduct.

A. "That was built about a hundred years ago."
Pause since no one knows what to say.
B. "I wonder how many bricks there are in it. There must be millions of course."
C. "Humph. Obviously."
B. "What I mean is, there must have been hundreds of men on the job . . . just on as much as we can see of it. Where did they live? Where are the nearest villages?"
A. "There's nothing for miles except two very tiny hamlets."
C. "Must have managed it somehow. Wonder how they managed to build at such an enormous height across the plain. . . ."

The conversation got under way, in spite of C's rather grumpy and discouraging grunt which nearly killed it at the outset. Notice how B introduced a human element which necessarily stirred interest, and how he developed it. When a few more exchanges had taken place he wisely brought in the topic of dry stone walling, that fascinating subject with its perpetual query as to how thousands of tons of stone were carried as walling over hundreds of miles of barren country.

B succeeded in speaking a little out of line with the subject of the viaduct and provided a channel for talk to flow along. He did this by an only moderately original viewpoint but, as Erasmus wrote somewhere or other, "Many people know this, but it has not occurred to many people's minds." No special knowledge is needed, but only an alert mind with an inquiring habit. Thus all you need will come, as Sir Thomas Browne says, "Not pickt from the leaves of an Author, but bred amongst the weeds and tares of mine own brain."

This chapter has outlined a code of conduct, a kind of etiquette, which will be serviceable as a background to the more definite rules earlier in the book. The points made build up an attitude of mind which is good and productive. They also encourage confidence, tolerance for others, and a friendliness of contact without which conversation is always severely handicapped. Thus is formed Cotton Mather's very pleasant and socially happy person,

> "A table-talker, rich in sense,
> And witty without wit's pretence."

If that sounds slightly formal, we may each of us at least be confident of possessing what Sidney Smith most cheerfully called, "a twelve-parson power of conversation".

CHAPTER X

EXERCISES FOR PRACTICE

EXPERIENCE in teaching the art of Conversation has shown that students derive the utmost benefit if they have a set of Exercises for private practice.

Without it they feel lost during the practical application of their lessons, just as they would feel if they were asked to take a solo flight after studying an aircraft manual. In this chapter, therefore, exercises and certain additional notes are given as a further personal aid for those who practise the principles which have been explained.

CHAPTER III

1. Write down the headings of a Thought Drift. Then write down in its entirety the full line of thought which follows from these items. That is, put down all the links between the headings you have noted, so that you are able to see exactly how your mind travelled from its starting point to the last heading.

   The purpose of this exercise is to give you opportunity to convince yourself that the method of Thought Drift is not an irresponsible jumping of the mind from point to point. You will see that it actually is a spontaneous and wholly natural method by which your mind, from any given starting point, will find its way forward through a logical sequence of ideas. This exercise will help you, at the beginning of your practice, to know that the method is a part of yourself. It is not something which you make your own, but definitely a bringing into your conscious control of a faculty which everyone possesses but of which most people are unaware.

2. Practise the Thought Drift three or four times daily. Note down the headings it provides for you, without troubling to record the links between each topic. This exercise will give you facility in discovering conversational topics by only the least possible initial effort. Soon you will find that you have formed a mental habit of noting these topics as your mind, by a normal reaction to the many things you observe in daily life, automatically selects them for you.

Notice that you should not try to *make* your mind think. It is supremely important that your mind should really drift. To set it to work, instead of allowing it to act for itself, is an interference in the job which it wishes to do naturally and without outside help. You should do no more than give it a starting point, an idea or an awareness of something outside itself, and then make a note of all the topics which it brings to your attention.

Do not at this stage attempt to use the Thought Drift in any serious conversation. While you are still practising the method of discovering conversational topics, be content to explore it thoroughly and to become easy and confident in your use of it.

Remember that after reading Chapter III you have still to learn how to make the best use of the topics which the Thought Drift provides. Without that instruction, you may easily find that you "run dry" soon after you have commenced your conversation. This is a discouragement you may well spare yourself by not using your topics while you are still practising the method of discovering them.

3. After you have become accustomed to letting your mind form its own Thought Drifts (this may take up three or four days of practice), you may start introducing their conversational topics into your talk. In doing this, it is advisable to talk to someone you know well, so that you may have the advantage of taking your first steps in the company of a person with whom you are at ease. Take care, however, not to develop any topic too far until you have studied Chapters IV and V.

CHAPTERS IV AND V

Practice of the lessons in these chapters should not be hurried. Moreover, you will find it an advantage to make up the exercises, to some extent, for yourself. This is because in the development of the Thought Drift topics each mind will work individually. To compel the individual to work through a fixed pattern of thinking would be harmful. Consequently you will see that the following exercises allow you the possibility of working yourself.

1. Form a Thought Drift about any or each of the following subjects. They are all abstract, and will thus incidentally enable you to develop your capacity for thinking and analysing topics.

The Seven Seas; Listening to the Radio; Books; Sport; Earning a Living; Gardening; The Necessity of Politics; Good Health; Imagination; One Hundred Years; Middle Life; Craftsmanship; Country Scenery; Happiness; Artificial Lighting; Travel; Fiction; Talking.

2. Select one conversational topic from a Thought
Drift based on a subject in the previous exercise.
Analyse it into its natural divisions.

As an example of this exercise, let us take a Thought
Drift which follows from the idea, *Colour*. This is sufficiently
abstract to give us opportunity to roam about in it. My
own Thought Drift deriving from *Colour* gives me the
following headings as possible topics of conversation:—
Variety — Meanings — Camouflage — Technical —
Manufacture—Shape—Mass—Nature.

Now let us analyse one of these ideas to see what
topics are revealed in a fairly fully developed stage of
preparation. Take the heading, *Variety*.

Without much effort your mind quickly divides the
idea into all that is contained in the further idea, *Colours
as party or political symbols, or as national colours*. This thought
breaks up at once, without effort on your part, into
detailed facts such as *Red for Communism, Green for Ireland*,
etc. Here we are able to pass from *Colour* associations to
quite independent topics, such as *political theory, nationalism,
patriotism*.

Each of these in turn more or less automatically divides
into further topics, so that what started as *Colour* and
became *Red for Communism* may become the three ideas,
*Individual Rights, Private Enterprise, Nationalisation of
Industry*.

Now let us go back to another of the headings in the
original Thought Drift on *Colour*, and let us analyse the
heading *Meanings*. On letting my mind dwell on it for a
few seconds I find that, although *Meanings* came into my
mind unexpectedly as a derivative from *Colour*, it none-
theless contains several ideas for me to choose from. Thus,

(*a*) What is Colour? How do I see Colour? Since a

thing has no colour if it is placed in a completely darkened room, how does it acquire colour when light is introduced? In brief, my topic here is *The Nature or Source of Colour*.

(*b*) Colour in Music. This idea pops into my mind, which knows little about it. This does not make me discard the topic as a possible means of conversation. It is most important that one should realise this fact. Since one aim of conversation is to enable others to talk, the fact that *Colour in Music* is a topic I can say almost nothing about may make it an extremely valuable subject if I am in the company of someone who is interested in it.

(*c*) Colour in Words. Here I find my mind has given me a topic I know something about—the power of words to convey an impression which is extra to the actual meaning in them. Thus the word "blare" has a suggestion of brightness in it, which is additional to its meaning.

These three ideas are interesting examples of what the mind will do for us in promoting conversation. We find that, in my own instance, it has provided a topic (*a*) which anyone can discuss; a topic (*b*) in which I would be an interested listener; and a topic (*c*) about which I could make my own contribution and about which I would also be interested to learn.

3. If you have not practised the final exercise for Chapter III, you should now do so. Previously it was suggested that you should limit your use of it, if you wished to experiment with it. Now, however, you are equipped to go as far as you find yourself able to carry on.

4. Foresee some occasion in business or social life when you may wish to persuade someone to accept your

viewpoint or act on your suggestion. Try to picture that person as you expect to meet him, e.g. in his sitting-room, his office, in a railway compartment. Allow your mind to form a Thought Drift which commences from something personal to him or close to him in those circumstances. When the Thought Drift is completely formed, shape it to your purpose by taking several of the topics it provides and giving them direction towards the accomplishment of that purpose, according to the means which Chapter V explained.

Write down the conversation which followed in your imaginative anticipation of the meeting. Wait for a day or two, and then examine the conversation to see how it might be improved as a means of securing the end you had in view.

From this exercise you can considerably improve your ability to persuade or to present your opinion convincingly.

CHAPTERS VI AND VII

In doing the following exercises be careful not to change the given examples into ponderous maxims. You are making epigrams, not composing moral sayings.

1. By changing one or two words only in each of these examples, make them express a different point of view.

> People usually give good advice when they can no longer give bad example.
>
> If you keep pulling on your oar, you are less likely to stick it into other people's business.
>
> The really great man is the man who makes other people feel great.
>
> Punctuality is the thief of Time.
>
> A crank is a little thing that makes revolutions.

2. It is often good practice to take a few words, as in the examples below, and complete them by adding not more than four or five words. This is useful in developing both facility and conciseness of expression. As an example, we may take the anonymous completion of words from one of Tom Moore's songs—"The love that lies in woman's eyes . . . and lies and lies."

What may be done in this way may also be exemplified by the old toast, "Sweethearts and wives—may they never meet!" Or we may consider the Rev. C. H. Spurgeon's, "A lie travels round the world—while Truth is putting on her boots."

In the same way, complete the following:—
    Remember the poor ......
    The lion has his mane, the peacock his gorgeous
        plumage, but Man found himself in ......
    Fear thy God, speak ill of none,
    Stick to the truth ......
    Knowledge is like a headstrong horse ......
    Earth has no sorrow that ......
    He that steals for others will ......
    The eye that sees all things else ......
    The man who sees both sides of a question ......
    Hope is a good breakfast but ......

CHAPTER VIII

Here are a few ideas about Anecdote which will set you, by way of exercise, to analysing stories and people and situations. This analysis, which obviously cannot be prescribed in advance, is valuable in aiding you to know when any particular anecdote is likely to be successful.

In a mixed company we may often be uncertain as to

whether any given story will be useful. This doubt arises not only because some people have a marked sense of humour while others are deficient in it, but also because we have no safe guide as to what humour actually is. We know the stories which make us laugh but this is not a guarantee that they will be effective when told to others. We need something more infallible than our own sense of humour if we are to be sure of choosing the right story to secure the effect we want in any conversation.

Probably we shall arrive at the most reliable conclusion if we examine the use of humorous anecdote, since what we learn from this is applicable to story-telling in general.

Experience and our own observation of the reactions of others to various stories will teach us a lot. In the meantime, there is one safe rule—that humour derives largely from one kind or another of what is unfitting. That is, incongruity makes almost everyone laugh. The world of comedy is occupied by a wide range of stock figures, many of whom we know well.

There is the stout man running to catch the bus, the player who gets his fingers trapped between the valves of his trumpet, the woman who says something completely *de trop*, the child who embarrasses his parents by some unconscious revelation of family gossip, the clergyman who makes an unfortunate mistake in his pulpit announcement. . . . The list could be continued almost indefinitely.

You have only to recall the celebrated cartoons of H. M. Bateman, about the man who coughed during a piano recital or cracked a nut during a soprano solo, to come straight to the heart of humour. Approaching from another angle, remember the delightful cartoons of Fougasse, who successfully exploits the incongruity between what people are saying and what they are doing, or, from yet another angle, by following the characteristics exhibited by David Langdon, who often shows us what we secretly think but never dare to say or do—as in the picture of the man who seats himself in the barber's chair and says, "Hair-cut, please, broken only by the busy snip-snip of scissors."

Incongruity in its truest and most subtle forms is the foundation on which rest those classics, *The Diary of a Nobody* by George and Weedon Grossmith, *My Life and Hard Times* by James Thurber, or the annals of Hyman Kaplan.

You will notice that in all these examples incongruity is not distortion. Mere oddity is not amusing. What is amusing, however, is something which appears to be odd but is in fact almost startlingly ordinary. It is the way in which the ordinary emerges which makes us laugh. We have all of us been guilty of "little jokes" no better than those which Mr. Pooter surprises himself by achieving in the domestic intimacy of The Little Laurels; what makes his successful is our knowledge that he isn't the kind of man who ever manages to say anything funny and original. His pun on the names of his friends, Cummings and Gowing, is apparent to the reader on first acquaintance, and it is too obvious to be amusing. In spite of this, when Pooter himself offends by telling his silly jokes the situation becomes funny.

What are we laughing at if not at the unexpectedness of this man's actually making a pun? Why are we amused by Kaplan's earnest endeavours to benefit by the tuition of his "Mr. Pockheel", unless it is because the man himself is wholly credible while his sayings are, granted the man, both inevitable and incongrous? We never know what he will say next, yet when he says it we cannot conceive his saying anything else.

We may take it, then, that humour to a large extent depends on a thing being incongruous yet credible even to the point of inevitability. This is equally true of a situation, a character, a saying, or an event.

What is unexpected is usually amusing, This is our surest guide as to whether a story will succeed, as do the lines

> "Here lie the remains of Mary Anne Chowder
> Who burst while taking a seidlitz powder . . ."

As an example, let us take a story which psychologists have offered as a test for establishing sense of humour.

Before reading it, you may be cautioned that in this setting it may not appear amusing, simply because the element of surprise has been largely taken away from it. We are considering it to see what "makes it tick" and few stories have a chance of amusing us when approached in this way. Here it is.

> The guest was deep in conversation with his hostess when he was asked whether he would take more cabbage. He did not hear the question. When asked for the second time, he took a handful of cabbage from the dish and rubbed it slowly into his hair. He then resumed conversation until the hostess, astounded at what he had done, interrupted him by asking, "Why did you rub cabbage into your hair?" The man looked astonished. He stared about him and then said, "I'm really sorry. To tell you the truth, I thought it was spinach."

THE UNEXPECTED SURPRISE

If you can tell that story without warning and afterwards ask people why they laughed at it, they will say it was because the story was so completely crazy. In actual fact, the improbability of the story is less responsible for their reaction than the unexpectedness of the jolt to their funny-bone.

An ordinary story follows a straight line. While we listen to it we are all the time trying to anticipate what the end will be. If there is an abrupt departure from the line we have been mentally forecasting, and the story takes a direction impossible to anticipate, we almost find that story interesting or even memorable. This is true whether the anecdote is humorous or not. The incongruity lies not so much in the thing told as in the way in which what actually happens differs from what we expected.

Our purpose here is sufficiently served if we note this fact, without troubling to go into the complex reasons why this is so.

Here is another classical story which contains the "essence" of good story-telling.

A man went into a bakery and asked whether he could order a cake made in the shape of the letter S. The baker assured him that he would be pleased to accept the order. "But you'll have to wait a week or so," he explained, "because I need to have a tin made for the job." "That's all right," said the man. "I don't mind how long I wait, provided the cake can be made." Some ten days later he walked into the bakery again and inquired about the cake. "You've come on the right day," said the baker. "We finished it last night." He showed the cake. To his surprise, the customer said, "I'm sorry, but this won't do. It's entirely my fault, because I should have told you that I wanted a cake in the shape of a small letter and not a capital one. I'll pay for this, but can you make me a cake just as I want it?" He was again assured that his request would be fulfilled, after another delay for the making of a special tin. A week later he called once more, inspected the cake, and expressed every satisfaction with it. The baker said, "Well, I have a box here for it, so I'll wrap it up. If you tell me the address, I'll deliver it for you." "Oh, don't worry about that," said the man. "If it's all the same to you, and if you lend me a knife, I'll eat it right here."

Now that story isn't really the least bit "crazy", although it seems to be on first hearing. It could have become wildly improbable but you will have noticed several little touches in it, here and there, which keep it straight all the way to the climax. Then it becomes wholly unexpected.

In these suggestions is to be found our guide in choosing a story to use as an illustration. When due consideration has been given to the factors to be remembered by a *raconteur*, such as the effective use of dialect, sound characterization, swiftness of action, appeal to the visual imagination, and so on, it is yet incontestable that the problem as to whether an anecdote is likely to be successful must be settled by the answer to the question . . . is the conclusion unexpected? If it is, the story will catch people's interest. And this makes a story worth while for the conversationalist. I will close by repeating—a story should never be told merely because it is a good story. Unless it advances the conversation, it is only entertainment. Its effect will be to turn a conversation into a recital of stories humorous or otherwise. This may provide an excellent way of enjoying people's company but it will destroy all hope of bringing about that blending of selves, that bringing out of the best which is in each mind and heart, which is the result of true conversation.

MELVIN POWERS SELF-IMPROVEMENT LIBRARY

ASTROLOGY
____ASTROLOGY—HOW TO CHART YOUR HOROSCOPE Max Heindel 7.00
____ASTROLOGY AND SEXUAL ANALYSIS Morris C. Goodman 7.00
____ASTROLOGY AND YOU Carroll Righter 5.00
____ASTROLOGY MADE EASY Astarte 7.00
____ASTROLOGY, ROMANCE, YOU AND THE STARS Anthony Norvell 10.00
____MY WORLD OF ASTROLOGY Sydney Omarr 10.00
____THOUGHT DIAL Sydney Omarr 7.00
____WHAT THE STARS REVEAL ABOUT THE MEN IN YOUR LIFE Thelma White 3.00

BRIDGE
____BRIDGE BIDDING MADE EASY Edwin B. Kantar 10.00
____BRIDGE CONVENTIONS Edwin B. Kantar 10.00
____COMPETITIVE BIDDING IN MODERN BRIDGE Edgar Kaplan 7.00
____DEFENSIVE BRIDGE PLAY COMPLETE Edwin B Kantar 20.00
____GAMESMAN BRIDGE—PLAY BETTER WITH KANTAR Edwin B. Kantar 7.00
____HOW TO IMPROVE YOUR BRIDGE Alfred Sheinwold 7.00
____IMPROVING YOUR BIDDING SKILLS Edwin B. Kantar 7.00
____INTRODUCTION TO DECLARER'S PLAY Edwin B. Kantar 7.00
____INTRODUCTION TO DEFENDER'S PLAY Edwin B. Kantar 7.00
____KANTAR FOR THE DEFENSE Edwin B. Kantar 7.00
____KANTAR FOR THE DEFENSE VOLUME 2 Edwin B. Kantar 7.00
____TEST YOUR BRIDGE PLAY Edwin B. Kantar 10.00
____VOLUME 2—TEST YOUR BRIDGE PLAY Edwin B. Kantar 10.00
____WINNING DECLARER PLAY Dorothy Hayden Truscott 10.00

BUSINESS, STUDY & REFERENCE
____BRAINSTORMING Charles Clark 10.00
____CONVERSATION MADE EASY Elliot Russell 5.00
____EXAM SECRET Dennis B. Jackson 5.00
____FIX-IT BOOK Arthur Symons 2.00
____HOW TO DEVELOP A BETTER SPEAKING VOICE M. Hellier 5.00
____HOW TO SAVE 50% ON GAS & CAR EXPENSES Ken Stansbie 5.00
____HOW TO SELF-PUBLISH YOUR BOOK & MAKE IT A BEST SELLER Melvin Powers . . 20.00
____INCREASE YOUR LEARNING POWER Geoffrey A. Dudley 5.00
____PRACTICAL GUIDE TO BETTER CONCENTRATION Melvin Powers 5.00
____PUBLIC SPEAKING MADE EASY Thomas Montalbo 10.00
____7 DAYS TO FASTER READING William S. Schaill 7.00
____SONGWRITER'S RHYMING DICTIONARY Jane Shaw Whitfield 10.00
____SPELLING MADE EASY Lester D. Basch & Dr. Milton Finkelstein 3.00
____STUDENT'S GUIDE TO BETTER GRADES J.A. Rickard 3.00
____TEST YOURSELF—FIND YOUR HIDDEN TALENT Jack Shafer 3.00
____YOUR WILL & WHAT TO DO ABOUT IT Attorney Samuel G. King 7.00

CALLIGRAPHY
____ADVANCED CALLIGRAPHY Katherine Jeffares 7.00
____CALLIGRAPHY—THE ART OF BEAUTIFUL WRITING Katherine Jeffares 7.00
____CALLIGRAPHY FOR FUN & PROFIT Anne Leptich & Jacque Evans 7.00
____CALLIGRAPHY MADE EASY Tina Serafini 7.00

CHESS & CHECKERS
____BEGINNER'S GUIDE TO WINNING CHESS Fred Reinfeld 7.00
____CHESS IN TEN EASY LESSONS Larry Evans 10.00
____CHESS MADE EASY Milton L. Hanauer 5.00
____CHESS PROBLEMS FOR BEGINNERS Edited by Fred Reinfeld 7.00

____CHESS TACTICS FOR BEGINNERS Edited by Fred Reinfeld 7.00
____HOW TO WIN AT CHECKERS Fred Reinfeld 5.00
____1001 BRILLIANT WAYS TO CHECKMATE Fred Reinfeld 10.00
____1001 WINNING CHESS SACRIFICES & COMBINATIONS Fred Reinfeld 10.00

COOKERY & HERBS
____CULPEPER'S HERBAL REMEDIES Dr. Nicholas Culpeper 5.00
____FAST GOURMET COOKBOOK Poppy Cannon 2.50
____HEALING POWER OF HERBS May Bethel 5.00
____HEALING POWER OF NATURAL FOODS May Bethel 7.00
____HERBS FOR HEALTH—HOW TO GROW & USE THEM Louise Evans Doole 7.00
____HOME GARDEN COOKBOOK—DELICIOUS NATURAL FOOD RECIPES Ken Kraft 3.00
____MEATLESS MEAL GUIDE Tomi Ryan & James H. Ryan, M.D. 4.00
____VEGETABLE GARDENING FOR BEGINNERS Hugh Wilberg 2.00
____VEGETABLES FOR TODAY'S GARDENS R. Milton Carleton 2.00
____VEGETARIAN COOKERY Janet Walker 10.00
____VEGETARIAN COOKING MADE EASY & DELECTABLE Veronica Vezza 3.00

GAMBLING & POKER
____HOW TO WIN AT POKER Terence Reese & Anthony T. Watkins 7.00
____SCARNE ON DICE John Scarne 15.00
____WINNING AT CRAPS Dr. Lloyd T. Commins 5.00
____WINNING AT GIN Chester Wander & Cy Rice 3.00
____WINNING AT POKER—AN EXPERT'S GUIDE John Archer 10.00
____WINNING AT 21—AN EXPERT'S GUIDE John Archer 10.00

HEALTH
____BEE POLLEN Lynda Lyngheim & Jack Scagnetti 5.00
____COPING WITH ALZHEIMER'S Rose Oliver, Ph.D. & Francis Bock, Ph.D. 10.00
____DR. LINDNER'S POINT SYSTEM FOOD PROGRAM Peter G Lindner, M.D. 2.00
____HELP YOURSELF TO BETTER SIGHT Margaret Darst Corbett 7.00
____HOW YOU CAN STOP SMOKING PERMANENTLY Ernest Caldwell 5.00
____MIND OVER PLATTER Peter G Lindner, M.D. 5.00
____NATURE'S WAY TO NUTRITION & VIBRANT HEALTH Robert J. Scrutton 3.00
____NEW CARBOHYDRATE DIET COUNTER Patti Lopez-Pereira 2.00
____REFLEXOLOGY Dr. Maybelle Segal 5.00
____REFLEXOLOGY FOR GOOD HEALTH Anna Kaye & Don C. Matchan 7.00
____30 DAYS TO BEAUTIFUL LEGS Dr. Marc Selner 3.00
____WONDER WITHIN Thomas S. Coyle, M.D. 10.00
____YOU CAN LEARN TO RELAX Dr. Samuel Gutwirth 5.00

HOBBIES
____BEACHCOMBING FOR BEGINNERS Norman Hickin 2.00
____BLACKSTONE'S MODERN CARD TRICKS Harry Blackstone 7.00
____BLACKSTONE'S SECRETS OF MAGIC Harry Blackstone 7.00
____COIN COLLECTING FOR BEGINNERS Burton Hobson & Fred Reinfeld 7.00
____ENTERTAINING WITH ESP Tony 'Doc' Shiels 2.00
____400 FASCINATING MAGIC TRICKS YOU CAN DO Howard Thurston 7.00
____HOW I TURN JUNK INTO FUN AND PROFIT Sari 3.00
____HOW TO WRITE A HIT SONG AND SELL IT Tommy Boyce 10.00
____MAGIC FOR ALL AGES Walter Gibson 7.00
____STAMP COLLECTING FOR BEGINNERS Burton Hobson 3.00

HORSE PLAYER'S WINNING GUIDES
____BETTING HORSES TO WIN Les Conklin 7.00
____ELIMINATE THE LOSERS Bob McKnight 5.00
____HOW TO PICK WINNING HORSES Bob McKnight 5.00
____HOW TO WIN AT THE RACES Sam (The Genius) Lewin 5.00
____HOW YOU CAN BEAT THE RACES Jack Kavanagh 5.00

_____ SEXUALLY FULFILLED MAN Dr. Rachel Copelan 5.00
_____ STAYING IN LOVE Dr. Norton F. Kristy 7.00

MELVIN POWERS'S MAIL ORDER LIBRARY
_____ HOW TO GET RICH IN MAIL ORDER Melvin Powers 20.00
_____ HOW TO SELF-PUBLISH YOUR BOOK Melvin Powers 20.00
_____ HOW TO WRITE A GOOD ADVERTISEMENT Victor O. Schwab 20.00
_____ MAIL ORDER MADE EASY J. Frank Brumbaugh 20.00
_____ MAKING MONEY WITH CLASSIFIED ADS Melvin Powers 20.00

METAPHYSICS & OCCULT
_____ CONCENTRATION—A GUIDE TO MENTAL MASTERY Mouni Sadhu 7.00
_____ EXTRA-TERRESTRIAL INTELLIGENCE—THE FIRST ENCOUNTER 6.00
_____ FORTUNE TELLING WITH CARDS P. Foli 5.00
_____ HOW TO INTERPRET DREAMS, OMENS & FORTUNE TELLING SIGNS Gettings 5.00
_____ HOW TO UNDERSTAND YOUR DREAMS Geoffrey A. Dudley 7.00
_____ MAGICIAN—HIS TRAINING AND WORK W.E. Butler 7.00
_____ MEDITATION Mouni Sadhu 10.00
_____ MODERN NUMEROLOGY Morris C. Goodman 5.00
_____ NUMEROLOGY—ITS FACTS AND SECRETS Ariel Yvon Taylor 5.00
_____ NUMEROLOGY MADE EASY W. Mykian 5.00
_____ PALMISTRY MADE EASY Fred Gettings 5.00
_____ PALMISTRY MADE PRACTICAL Elizabeth Daniels Squire 7.00
_____ PROPHECY IN OUR TIME Martin Ebon 2.50
_____ SUPERSTITION—ARE YOU SUPERSTITIOUS? Eric Maple 2.00
_____ TAROT Mouni Sadhu 10.00
_____ TAROT OF THE BOHEMIANS Papus 10.00
_____ WAYS TO SELF-REALIZATION Mouni Sadhu 7.00
_____ WITCHCRAFT, MAGIC & OCCULTISM—A FASCINATING HISTORY W.B. Crow 10.00
_____ WITCHCRAFT—THE SIXTH SENSE Justine Glass 7.00

RECOVERY
_____ KNIGHT IN RUSTY ARMOR Robert Fisher 5.00
_____ KNIGHT IN RUSTY ARMOR (Hard cover edition) Robert Fisher 10.00
_____ KNIGHTS WITHOUT ARMOR (Hard cover edition) Aaron R. Kipnis, Ph.D. 10.00
_____ PRINCESS WHO BELIEVED IN FAIRY TALES Marcia Grad 10.00

SELF-HELP & INSPIRATIONAL
_____ CHARISMA—HOW TO GET "THAT SPECIAL MAGIC" Marcia Grad 10.00
_____ DAILY POWER FOR JOYFUL LIVING Dr. Donald Curtis 7.00
_____ DYNAMIC THINKING Melvin Powers 5.00
_____ GREATEST POWER IN THE UNIVERSE U.S. Andersen 10.00
_____ GROW RICH WHILE YOU SLEEP Ben Sweetland 10.00
_____ GROW RICH WITH YOUR MILLION DOLLAR MIND Brian Adams 7.00
_____ GROWTH THROUGH REASON Albert Ellis, Ph.D. 10.00
_____ GUIDE TO PERSONAL HAPPINESS Albert Ellis, Ph.D. & Irving Becker, Ed.D. 10.00
_____ HANDWRITING ANALYSIS MADE EASY John Marley 10.00
_____ HANDWRITING TELLS Nadya Olyanova 7.00
_____ HOW TO ATTRACT GOOD LUCK A.H.Z. Carr 7.00
_____ HOW TO DEVELOP A WINNING PERSONALITY Martin Panzer 7.00
_____ HOW TO DEVELOP AN EXCEPTIONAL MEMORY Young & Gibson 10.00
_____ HOW TO LIVE WITH A NEUROTIC Albert Ellis, Ph.D. 10.00
_____ HOW TO OVERCOME YOUR FEARS M.P. Leahy, M.D. 3.00
_____ HOW TO SUCCEED Brian Adams 7.00
_____ HUMAN PROBLEMS & HOW TO SOLVE THEM Dr. Donald Curtis 5.00
_____ I CAN Ben Sweetland 8.00
_____ I WILL Ben Sweetland 10.00
_____ KNIGHT IN RUSTY ARMOR Robert Fisher 5.00
_____ KNIGHT IN RUSTY ARMOR (Hard Cover) Robert Fisher 10.00

___ LEFT-HANDED PEOPLE Michael Barsley 5.00
___ MAGIC IN YOUR MIND U.S. Andersen 10.00
___ MAGIC OF THINKING SUCCESS Dr. David J. Schwartz 8.00
___ MAGIC POWER OF YOUR MIND Walter M. Germain 10.00
___ MENTAL POWER THROUGH SLEEP SUGGESTION Melvin Powers 3.00
___ NEVER UNDERESTIMATE THE SELLING POWER OF A WOMAN Dottie Walters 7.00
___ NEW GUIDE TO RATIONAL LIVING Albert Ellis, Ph.D. & R. Harper, Ph.D. 10.00
___ PRINCESS WHO BELIEVED IN FAIRY TALES Marcia Grad 10.00
___ PSYCHO-CYBERNETICS Maxwell Maltz, M.D. 10.00
___ PSYCHOLOGY OF HANDWRITING Nadya Olyanova 7.00
___ SALES CYBERNETICS Brian Adams 10.00
___ SCIENCE OF MIND IN DAILY LIVING Dr. Donald Curtis 7.00
___ SECRET OF SECRETS U.S. Andersen 7.00
___ SECRET POWER OF THE PYRAMIDS U.S. Andersen 7.00
___ SELF-THERAPY FOR THE STUTTERER Malcolm Frazer 3.00
___ SUCCESS CYBERNETICS U.S. Andersen 7.00
___ 10 DAYS TO A GREAT NEW LIFE William E. Edwards 3.00
___ THINK AND GROW RICH Napoleon Hill 10.00
___ THINK LIKE A WINNER Walter Doyle Staples, Ph.D. 10.00
___ THREE MAGIC WORDS U.S. Andersen 10.00
___ TREASURY OF COMFORT Edited by Rabbi Sidney Greenberg 10.00
___ TREASURY OF THE ART OF LIVING Sidney S. Greenberg 10.00
___ WHAT YOUR HANDWRITING REVEALS Albert E. Hughes 4.00
___ WONDER WITHIN Thomas F. Coyle, M.D. 10.00
___ YOUR SUBCONSCIOUS POWER Charles M. Simmons 7.00
___ YOUR THOUGHTS CAN CHANGE YOUR LIFE Dr. Donald Curtis 7.00

SPORTS

___ BILLIARDS—POCKET • CAROM • THREE CUSHION Clive Cottingham, Jr. 7.00
___ COMPLETE GUIDE TO FISHING Vlad Evanoff 2.00
___ HOW TO IMPROVE YOUR RACQUETBALL Lubarsky, Kaufman & Scagnetti 5.00
___ HOW TO WIN AT POCKET BILLIARDS Edward D. Knuchell 10.00
___ JOY OF WALKING Jack Scagnetti 3.00
___ LEARNING & TEACHING SOCCER SKILLS Eric Worthington 3.00
___ RACQUETBALL FOR WOMEN Toni Hudson, Jack Scagnetti & Vince Rondone 3.00
___ SECRET OF BOWLING STRIKES Dawson Taylor 5.00
___ SOCCER—THE GAME & HOW TO PLAY IT Gary Rosenthal 7.00
___ STARTING SOCCER Edward F Dolan, Jr. 5.00

TENNIS LOVER'S LIBRARY

___ HOW TO BEAT BETTER TENNIS PLAYERS Loring Fiske 4.00
___ PSYCH YOURSELF TO BETTER TENNIS Dr. Walter A. Luszki 2.00
___ TENNIS FOR BEGINNERS Dr. H.A. Murray 2.00
___ TENNIS MADE EASY Joel Brecheen 5.00
___ WEEKEND TENNIS—HOW TO HAVE FUN & WIN AT THE SAME TIME Bill Talbert ... 3.00

WILSHIRE PET LIBRARY

___ DOG TRAINING MADE EASY & FUN John W. Kellogg 5.00
___ HOW TO BRING UP YOUR PET DOG Kurt Unkelbach 2.00
___ HOW TO RAISE & TRAIN YOUR PUPPY Jeff Griffen 5.00

The books listed above can be obtained from your book dealer or directly from Melvin Powers.
When ordering, please remit $2.00 postage for the first book and $1.00 for each additional book.

Melvin Powers
12015 Sherman Road, No. Hollywood, California 91605

WILSHIRE HORSE LOVERS' LIBRARY

___ AMATEUR HORSE BREEDER A.C. Leighton Hardman 5.00
___ AMERICAN QUARTER HORSE IN PICTURES Margaret Cabel Self 5.00
___ APPALOOSA HORSE Donna & Bill Richardson 7.00
___ ARABIAN HORSE Reginald S. Summerhays 7.00
___ ART OF WESTERN RIDING Suzanne Norton Jones 7.00
___ BASIC DRESSAGE Jean Froissard 7.00
___ BEGINNER'S GUIDE TO HORSEBACK RIDING Sheila Wall 5.00
___ BITS—THEIR HISTORY, USE AND MISUSE Louis Taylor 10.00
___ BREAKING & TRAINING THE DRIVING HORSE Doris Ganton 10.00
___ BREAKING YOUR HORSE'S BAD HABITS W. Dayton Sumner 10.00
___ COMPLETE TRAINING OF HORSE AND RIDER Colonel Alois Podhajsky 10.00
___ DISORDERS OF THE HORSE & WHAT TO DO ABOUT THEM E. Hanauer 5.00
___ DOG TRAINING MADE EASY AND FUN John W. Kellogg 5.00
___ DRESSAGE—A STUDY OF THE FINER POINTS IN RIDING Henry Wynmalen 7.00
___ DRIVE ON Doris Ganton 7.00
___ DRIVING HORSES Sallie Walrond 7.00
___ EQUITATION Jean Froissard 7.00
___ FIRST AID FOR HORSES Dr. Charles H. Denning, Jr. 5.00
___ FUN ON HORSEBACK Margaret Cabell Self 4.00
___ HORSE DISEASES—CAUSES, SYMPTOMS & TREATMENT Dr. H.G. Belschner 7.00
___ HORSE OWNER'S CONCISE GUIDE Elsie V. Hanauer 5.00
___ HORSE SELECTION & CARE FOR BEGINNERS George H. Conn 10.00
___ HORSEBACK RIDING FOR BEGINNERS Louis Taylor 10.00
___ HORSEBACK RIDING MADE EASY & FUN Sue Henderson Coen 7.00
___ HORSES—THEIR SELECTION, CARE & HANDLING Margaret Cabell Self 5.00
___ HOW TO CURE BEHAVIOR PROBLEMS IN HORSES Susan McBane 15.00
___ HUNTER IN PICTURES Margaret Cabell Self 2.00
___ ILLUSTRATED BOOK OF THE HORSE S. Sidney (8½" x 11") 10.00
___ ILLUSTRATED HORSEBACK RIDING FOR BEGINNERS Jeanne Mellin 5.00
___ KNOW ALL ABOUT HORSES Harry Disston 5.00
___ LAME HORSE—CAUSES, SYMPTOMS & TREATMENT Dr. James R. Rooney 10.00
___ LAW & YOUR HORSE Edward H. Greene 7.00
___ POLICE HORSES Judith Campbell 2.00
___ PRACTICAL GUIDE TO HORSESHOEING 5.00
___ PRACTICAL HORSE PSYCHOLOGY Moyra Williams 7.00
___ PROBLEM HORSES—CURING SERIOUS BEHAVIOR HABITS Summerhays 5.00
___ REINSMAN OF THE WEST—BRIDLES & BITS Ed Connell 7.00
___ RIDE WESTERN Louis Taylor 7.00
___ SCHOOLING YOUR YOUNG HORSE George Wheatley 7.00
___ STABLE MANAGEMENT FOR THE OWNER—GROOM George Wheatley 7.00
___ STALLION MANAGEMENT—A GUIDE FOR STUD OWNERS A.C. Hardman 5.00
___ YOU AND YOUR PONY Pepper Mainwaring Healey (8½" x 11") 6.00
___ YOUR PONY BOOK Hermann Wiederhold 2.00

The books listed above can be obtained from your book dealer or directly from Melvin Powers. When ordering, please remit $2.00 postage for the first book and $1.00 for each additional book.

Melvin Powers
12015 Sherman Road, No. Hollywood, California 91605

Notes

Notes

Notes